A Nation Under God

By

Ken Clifton

A Nation Under God
ISBN: 978-0-557-11839-7

Copyright © 2009 by Ken Clifton
writingken@yahoo.com
http://www.myspace.com/kenclifton

All Scriptures from the King James Version of the bible and may be
freely quoted and distributed.

A Nation Under God

Table of Contents

Introduction   i
State recognition of God   3
  -State constitutions and Thanksgiving proclamations
  providing acknowledgement of God by all 50 states.

Presidential recognition of God   52
  -Inaugural Addresses and other speeches by Presidents
  officially acknowledging God.

An American Religious Heritage   90
  -Examples in our nation's history of reliance upon the
  Lord's providential hand in times of need and prosperity.

Religion in Government Today   107
  -A sampling of public displays of religious expression
  in various locations and governmental extensions.

Why They Believed – 100 Scriptures of Trust   119
  -100 Scriptures containing the word "trust" in them,
  revealing the benefits and blessings of trusting God.

Source Citations and Research Links   143
  -Sources for the texts in the book, as well as web links
  for further research.

Introduction

This is the updated version of this book to include the words of our current President, Barack Obama. Now, I must admit that I felt this leader wasn't God's choice in the election and didn't feel like doing an update of this book, at first. There are many reasons to be cautious about this leader, including his failure to establish a denomination in over a year or attend church service in that time (prompting me to classify him as non-denominational). However, I've come to realize that God can operate through anyone. David would not attack Saul, even though Saul sought his life. Jesus told Pilate that God had given him power to rule. Also, in 1 Tim. 2:2 it says to pray for those in power over you, so you may have peace. I didn't get that, at first. However, I do, now. Although we are not entitled to pray for just anyone (their faith or lack of it will determine their future), we are SPECIFICALLY instructed to pray for our leaders. When they accept office over us, we are empowered to pray all demonic and evil influence away from them, so they may decide with God's wisdom the challenges we face....no matter the party or their faith choice. By winning the election, they empower us to pray for them for our benefit. So, pray for the President and Congressional leaders. We are still A NATION UNDER GOD!

-Intro from Last Editions-

In the reading the words of our nation's fathers, I feel that I am among heroes. How is it that we have lost their passion for righteousness, their love for family, and their firm reliance upon the Lord? Maybe, we lost it in the quick pace of life or, perhaps, in the advancement of the technical, we have forgotten the practical. George Washington said that God's providential hand "can supply every human defect." Yet, do we seek that hand?

i

Benjamin Franklin, in the Constitutional Convention, pointed out God's providential hand at work in the American Revolution and, then, said, "And have we now forgotten that powerful friend?" This question could, as well, be posed to each one of us. Today, we woke up in a land of freedom that was won by religious men. We have life by God's Hand, and He is the author of all that is good in our lives; however, do we say a thank you? Do we even acknowledge His provision?

Proverbs 3:5-6 says, "Trust in the LORD with all thine heart; and lean not unto thine own understanding. In all thy ways acknowledge him, and he shall direct thy paths."

Our founders knew how to acknowledge the Lord. In this book you will find words of devotion by Presidents, Governors, and nation-founders, as well as common men and women, showing the breadth and depth of our nation's trust in the Lord.

Our national religious history's tapestry contains many strong threads of thanksgiving. From founders to Presidents to state proclamations, our nation has offered up many prayers of thanks for the blessings that He has poured out upon us all.

You see, our founders knew something that we should learn in this age of terror and security issues. As Franklin Pierce said, "It must be felt that there is no national security but in the nation's humble, acknowledged dependence upon God and His overruling providence." Even with our best defense and strongest attempts to secure, the enemy may still get through. Why? It is because we do not know who all of our enemies are, where they are, or what they are doing. However, the Lord is all-knowing. There is not one evil intention that has arisen that the Lord has not known would occur since creation. We would be fools to not seek this all-knowing and all-powerful friend in the life of our nation.

Benjamin Franklin said, "God governs in the affairs of men." God will act in the life of our nation, by act or omission - blessing or cursing. The choice is up to us as to how we want that response to be. Even Adam Smith spoke of the "invisible hand" at work in our economy. How do we want that hand to operate, in support or opposition?

In wars, peace, national expansion and industrial growth, our nation has a history of reliance upon the Lord. You will see in reading these texts that faith and providence were not by-words to the individuals that established our Land. They were a lifeblood of their existence. They were the foundation upon which our nation was built, and shall we let that foundation falter now, when we need it the most.

My hope in this book is that we would learn from our history and heritage the value of trust in the Lord, so that we may reap the benefits of a nation "under God."

"I assume this trust in the humility of knowledge that only through the guidance of Almighty Providence can I hope to discharge its ever-increasing burdens." – Herbert Hoover

State Recognition of God

Over the course of time, each state of the United States of America has officially acknowledged God, many of them doing so many different times. God's Name was no byword or unimportant tradition to them. They knew the comfort and potential that could be found in God's unseen hand at work on their behalf.

In the pages that follows, you'll find God being acknowledged and petitioned by Governors or constitutions of each of the fifty states, showing the breadth and depth of our national religious heritage.

As I pointed out, many states acknowledged God many different times; however, for space and form, I have limited myself to one proclamation per state. In some cases, there is both a constitutional quote and a proclamation.

In choosing the proclamations, I preferred those from earlier decades and centuries in our history. Just imagine the early days of westward expansion. Citizens would pack up all that they could fit on their wagon and set out to establish our nation. They faced wild animals, fierce storms, native attackers, and more. These pioneers understood their dependence upon God's protective and providential hand.

In this day of excess, waste and pride, may we learn from the heritage of dependence upon God of our states, so that we may, as well, feel God's smiles over us.

Alabama – 22nd state
State Motto: "We Dare Defend Our Rights"

<u>Alabama State Constitution</u>:

PREAMBLE
We, the people of the State of Alabama, in order to establish justice, insure domestic tranquillity, and secure the blessings of liberty to ourselves and our posterity, invoking the favor and guidance of Almighty God, do ordain and establish the following Constitution and form of government for the State of Alabama...

SECTION 1
Equality and rights of men

That all men are equally free and independent; that they are endowed by their Creator with certain inalienable rights; that among these are life, liberty and the pursuit of happiness.

Alaska - 49th state
State Motto: "North to the Future"

<u>Alaska State Constitution</u>:

Preamble:
We the people of Alaska, grateful to God and to those who founded our nation and pioneered this great land, in order to secure and transmit to succeeding generations our heritage of political, civil, and religious liberty within the Union of States, do ordain and establish this constitution for the State of Alaska.

Arizona - 48th state
State Motto: "Diat Deus"
(God enriches)

Proclamation of Thanksgiving –1904

The closing of a year of exceptional prosperity and plenty brings to the people of Arizona an opportunity to express their unfaltering faith in the beneficence of Almighty God, and it is with an abiding trust that we again welcome the season of Thanksgiving.

Let it bring to our minds in grateful acknowledgment all the blessings that have come to us; let us be thankful that the general health of the people of Arizona has been good, that our mines, fields and forests have yielded abundantly, that in all lines of industry our people have prospered, and honest toil and endeavor have been richly rewarded, leading to the contentment of all.

In recognition of the many gifts of Providence, I, ALEXANDER O. BRODIE, Governor of the Territory of Arizona, do hereby recommend, in conformity with the proclamation of the President of the United States, that THURSDAY, OCTOBER 24, 1904, be observed throughout the Territory by devotion to Thanksgiving and prayer, remembering those who are in need by acts of Christian charity and brotherly love, thus proving our worthiness of the Divine blessings of Almighty God.

In witness whereof, I have hereunto set my hand, and caused the Great Seal of the Territory of Arizona to be affixed. Done at the Capitol, in the City of Phoenix, this eleventh day of November, A. D. 1904.

Arkansas - 25th state
State Motto: "Regnat Populus"
(The People Rule)

A Nation Under God

<u>Arkansas State Constitution</u>:

Preamble:
We, the people of the State of Arkansas, grateful to Almighty God for the privilege of choosing our own form of government, for our civil and religious liberty, and desiring to perpetuate its blessings and secure the same to our selves and posterity, do ordain and establish this Constitution.

Sec. 25. Protection of religion.
Religion, morality and knowledge being essential to good government, the General Assembly shall enact suitable laws to protect every religious denomination in the peaceable enjoyment of its own mode of public worship.

California - 31st state
State Motto: "Eureka"
(I Have Found It)

<u>Thanksgiving proclamation – 1904</u>

Whereas, The people of the State of California are peculiarly blessed in a beautiful land, favored beyond measure--a land where the best things of every clime are plenteously at hand, and Providence has guided us to build here a commonwealth founded firm in the principles of Magna Charta and the moral law, so that to-day we are a contented people, secure in our liberties, sane and God-fearing in our daily life, without disastrous inner dissensions or class strife, and amenable at all times to the dictates of justice and the rules of fair dealing; and,
Whereas, We have had during the past year bountiful harvests of many kinds, our varied manufacturing industries are prospering, and our material welfare generally is greater than ever before, with possibilities more hopeful and alluring than those vouchsafed to any other people wheresoever situated; and,

6

Whereas, We realize that all we are and all we have as a people is by favor of the all-loving God, whose continuous care is the basis of our welfare.

Now, Therefore, I, George C. Pardee, Governor of the State of California, in accordance with custom and with the proclamation of the President of the United States, do hereby appoint and set apart Thursday, the twenty-fourth day of November, A. D. 1904, as a Public Holiday, on which day all public and all but the most necessary private business should be laid aside, in order that our people may have opportunity to offer up their thanks to God for His past mercies, and, as one people, supplicate for the continuance of His favors.

In Witness Whereof, I have hereunto set my hand and caused the Great Seal of State to be hereunto affixed at the city of Sacramento, California, this fifth day of November, nineteen hundred and four.

Colorado - 38th state
State Motto: "Nil Sine Numine"
(Nothing Without Providence)

Colorado State Constitution:

Preamble:

We, the people of Colorado, with profound reverence for the Supreme Ruler of the Universe, in order to form a more independent and perfect government; establish justice; insure tranquility; provide for the common defense; promote the general welfare and secure the blessings of liberty to ourselves and our posterity, do ordain and establish this constitution for the "State of Colorado".

Connecticut - 5th state
State Motto: "Qui Transtulit Sustinet"
(He Who Transplanted Still Sustains)

Thanksgiving Proclamation - 1842

Gratitude to Almighty God for His manifold blessings, both spiritual and temporal, is the first and highest duty of intelligent beings.

I do, therefore, recommend that Thursday, the seventeenth day of November next, be observed by the people of this State as a day of Christian Thanksgiving and Prayer; and I do invite them, on that day, to render to their Almighty and Beneficent Father the sincere homage of fervent and grateful hearts, for His never ending goodness, not only by appropriate religious exercises in their temples of public worship, but by feeding the hungry, clothing the naked, visiting the sick, and administering consolation to the afflicted.

Given under my Hand and the Seal of the State, at Hampton, this eighteenth day of October, in the year of our Lord one thousand eight hundred and forty-two, and of the Independence of the United States of America the sixty-seventh.

Delaware - 1st state
State Motto: "Liberty and Independence"

Thanksgiving Proclamation - 1910

Ever mindful of the Source whence come all our blessings, we lift up our hearts in gratitude to Almighty God for His goodness and mercy.

The passing year came with the blossom of promise, and has lavished upon us the bloom of fulfillment. Health and prosperity have blessed the people. The homes have abounded in rich content. The various industries have flourished. The fields have smiled a golden harvest.

And therefore, in recognition of His faithful care, as well as in conformity with the recommendation of the President of the United States. I, Simeon S. Pennewill, Governor of the State of Delaware, do set apart Thursday, November 24th instant, as a Day of Thanksgiving and Prayer; and do recommend that the people of this State on that day refrain from their usual vocations, and in their homes and places of worship, render thanks unto God for His manifold blessings, and prayers for the continuance of His Divine favors.

Florida - 27th state
State Motto: "In God We Trust"

Thanksgiving Proclamation – 1904

GOD, in His infinite goodness and mercy, has so bountifully blessed the people of Florida that it is meet that we should devote a day to sincere prayer and thanksgiving to Him for the blessings that He has vouchsafed to us in continued health, abundant harvests and steadily increasing prosperity. Under His guidance we are rapidly developing the resources of our fields and forests, our mines and the waters in and around our State, and His care has shielded us from plague and pestilence and from great disasters of fire and flood. He has made the blessed rains to fall on the land, and the storms to pass us by unharmed. The enterprises to which we have turned our hands have yielded rich returns and all classes and conditions of our people are prospering as never before in our history. The universal contentment of citizenship, the happy course of our public affairs in general are evidences of Divine beneficence toward us.

Our forefathers, recognizing the hand of the Almighty in the blessings accorded them, established this beautiful and purely American custom of devoting one day especially set apart to thanksgiving and praise. Adopted by each succeeding generation, it has become a sacred and beautiful obligation to acknowledge our duty to the Giver of all good and to devoutly supplicate their gracious continuance in the future.

Now, therefore, in conformity with the established custom and with the proclamation of the President of the United States of America, I, William J. Jennings, Governor of the State of Florida, do most earnestly recommend the observance of Thursday, the 24th day of November, A. D. 1904, as a day of thanksgiving and praise to the Great Ruler of the Universe for His mercy and goodness to our State and our people. On that day let us lay aside our business affairs, repair to our usual place of worship and there give earnest and hearty thanks to God for the blessing of good government, good health, good harvests and the rich prosperity so bounteously bestowed upon us. And at the same time humbly and fervently beseech Him to preserve us from the arrogance of prosperity; to imprint upon our hearts a deep and solemn sense of our obligations to Him for them; to remit all our offenses and to incline us by His Holy Spirit to that sincere repentance and reformation which may afford us reason to hope for His inestimable favor, and that the blessings of peace, freedom and pure religion may be speedily extended to all nations of the earth.

In witness whereof, I have hereunto set my hand and caused the Great Seal of the State of Florida to be affixed. Done in the City of Tallahassee this the twelfth day of November, in the year of our Lord one thousand nine hundred and four, and of the independence of the United States the one hundred and twenty-ninth.

Georgia - 4th state
State Motto: "Wisdom, Justice, and Moderation"

Georgia Colony Thanksgiving Proclamation – 1742

ALMIGHTY GOD hath in all Ages shown His Power and

Mercy in the Miraculous and Gracious Deliverance of His Church, and in the Protection of Righteous and Religious Kings, and States professing His holy and eternal Truth, from the open Invasions, wicked Conspiracies and malicious Practices, of all the Enemies thereof. He hath by the Manifestation of His Providence delivered us from the hands of the Spaniards, they with fourteen Sail of small Gallies and other Craft came into Cumberland Sound; but Fear and Terror from the Lord, came upon them and they fleed. The Spaniards also, with another mighty Fleet of 36 Ships and Vessels came into Jekyll Sound, and after a sharp Fight became Masters thereof; we having only four Vessels to oppose their whole Force, and GOD was the Shield of our People. Since in so unequal a Fight, which was stoutly maintained for the space of four Hours, not one of ours was killed, though many of theirs Perished, and five were killed by one Shot only. They Landed 4500 Men upon this Island, according to the Accounts of the Prisoners, and even of Englishmen who escaped from them. The first Party Marchal up thro' the Woods to this Town, and was within sight thereof, when God delivered them into the Hands of a few of ours. They Fought and were dispersed and fleed. Another Party which supported them also Fought, but were soon dispersed. We may with Truth say, that the Hand of the Lord Fought for us; for in the two Fights more than 500 fleed before 50, and yet they for a time Fought with Courage, and the Granadiers particularly, charged with great Resolution, but their Shot did not take Place, in so much that none of ours were killed; but they were broken and pursued with great Slaughter, so that by the Reports of the Prisoners, since taken, upwards of 200 Men never returned to their Camp. They also cane up with their half Gallies towards this Town, and retired without so much as Firing one Shot, and then Fear came upon them and they fleed, leaving behind them some Cannon, and many Things they had taken. Twenty Eight Sail attacked Fort William, in which was only 50 Men, and after three Hours Fight, went away, and left the Province: They having been pursued as far as St. John's so that by this whole Expedition and great Armaments, no more than two of ours were taken and 2 killed. Therefore with Truth we may say, that the Lord hath done great Things for us, who hath delivered us out of the Hands of a Numerous Enemy; who had already Swallowed us up in their Thoughts and boasted that they would Torture and

Burn us. But the Lord was our Shield, and we of a Truth may say, that it was not our Strength nor Might that delivered us, but that it was the Lord; Therefore it is Meat and Fitting, that we should return Thanks unto God our Deliverer.

HAVING taken the Premisses into Consideration, I do hereby Order that Sunday the 25th Instant be observed as a Day of publick Thanksgiving to Almighty God for his great deliverance in having put an End to the Spanish Invasion, and that all Persons do Solemnize the same in a Christian and Religious Manner, and abstain from Drunkenness and any other wicked or dissolate Testimonies of Joy.

GIVEN under my Hand and Seal, this 24th Day of July, at Frederica in Georgia, Anno Domini 1742.

Hawaii - 50th state
State Motto: "The Life of the Land Is Perpetuated in Righteousness"

Hawaii State Constitution:

Preamble:
We, the people of Hawaii, grateful for Divine Guidance, and mindful of our Hawaiian heritage and uniqueness as an island State, dedicate our efforts to fulfill the philosophy decreed by the Hawaii State motto, "Ua mau ke ea o ka aina i ka pono."

We reserve the right to control our destiny, to nurture the integrity of our people and culture, and to preserve the quality of life that we desire.

We reaffirm our belief in a government of the people, by the people and for the people, and with an understanding and compassionate heart toward all the peoples of the earth, do hereby ordain and establish this constitution for the State of Hawaii. [Am Const Con 1978 and election Nov 7, 1978]

Idaho - 43ʳᵈ state
State Motto: "Esto Perpetua"
(May It Endure Forever)

Thanksgiving Proclamation - 1879

In civilized nations, special days are consecrated to memorable events--victories, deliverances, Divine benefactions:--days of congratulation and of sorrow:--days which measure epochs in discovery, invention, intellectual advance, moral growth and social change:--days to mark the succession of seasons, and to celebrate, in grateful observances, the blessings which they bring.

It has been a custom from the early times, at the falling of the leaf, when the ripened fruits of toil are gathered, to pause and reverently thank God for His goodness and care. Recognizing the fitness of this observance, at the close of a year crowned with peace, plenty and tranquility, The President has, by Proclamation, set apart THURSDAY, THE TWENTY-SEVENTH DAY OF THIS MONTH OF NOVEMBER, for the giving of "thanks and praise to ALMIGHTY GOD for His mercies, and to devoutly beseech their continuance."

In full sympathy with this act of National consecration, it is recommended to the good People of Idaho, that they remit their accustomed labors, and devote the day to the public services of religion, in their chosen ways--to the assembling of families--to the strengthening of kindred and social ties--to the forgiveness of injuries, and to the rational enjoyment of those temporal blessings which have fallen from the Divine hand.

On that day may the stranger find a welcome at our tables, our firesides and altars; and comfort and consolation be brought to the children of want and sorrow, on whom the chastening hand has been laid.

Mingled with all thankfulness for the past, and joy in the present, let there be fervent supplication, that righteousness may so exalt this Nation, that it shall be held in honor and fear throughout the earth--that the union of these States may be perpetual--that strifes and jealousies may cease--that, animated by love of our country and kind, we may realize "How good and

13

how pleasant it is for brethren to dwell together in unity."

Given under my hand and the Great Seal of Idaho Territory, at Boise City, this tenth day of November, in the year of our Lord one thousand eight hundred and seventy-nine, and of the Independence of the United States, the one hundred and fourth.

Illinois - 21ˢᵗ state
State Motto: "State Sovereignty – National Union"

Thanksgiving Proclamation - 1906

THE PRESIDENT of the United States having by proclamation designated Thursday, November twenty-ninth, nineteen hundred and six, as a national day of Thanksgiving,

Now, Therefore, I, CHARLES S. DENEEN, Governor of the State of Illinois, do hereby urge upon our citizens the setting apart of that day for the returning of thanks for the abundance with which we have been blessed by Providence during the past year. Not only has our material prosperity been unbounded, but the closing year has been one of peace throughout the State and Nation. The blessings which flow from the maintenance of social order are more and more appreciated by our citizens, and higher standards of individual and official integrity are constantly demanded. The truth that, along with the privileges of free institutions, go corresponding obligations, responsibilities and duties, is growing better understood, and to these, through the peaceful discipline of an orderly social life, our citizens are learning more and more readily to respond.

For these manifold social and material blessings, we as a people should be grateful, and the observance of Thanksgiving Day should be but the natural outpouring of our hearts in gratitude to the Bountiful Giver of the harvest and of the liberty and enlightenment which He has made our portion as a state and nation.

IN TESTIMONY WHEREOF, I have hereunto set my hand and caused to be affixed the Great Seal of State, this twelfth day of November, Anno Domini nineteen hundred and six.

Indiana - 19th state
State Motto: "Crossroads of America"

Indiana State Constitution:

Preamble:
TO THE END, that justice be established, public order maintained, and liberty perpetuated; WE, the People of the State of Indiana, grateful to ALMIGHTY GOD for the free exercise of the right to choose our own form of government, do ordain this Constitution.

ARTICLE 1. Bill of Rights

Section 1. WE DECLARE, That all people are created equal; that they are endowed by their CREATOR with certain inalienable rights...

Iowa - 29th state
State Motto: "Our Liberties We Prize and Our Rights We Will Maintain"

Thanksgiving Proclamation – 1864

15

WHEREAS, It has pleased Almighty God to vouchsafe unto us as a Nation and People manifold blessings throughout another year, and a day for NATIONAL THANKSGIVING has been designated by the President of the United States, and

WHEREAS, The State of Iowa has shared the full degree of Divine favor in this, that there is peace and plenty within her borders, her people healthful and prosperous, and their devotion to Liberty and the Union unalterable--

THEREFORE, I. William M. Stone, Governor of the State of Iowa, in pursuance of a time honored custom, do, by this my Proclamation, make known that THURSDAY, NOVEMBER 24TH, 1864, the day set apart by the President for grateful acknowledgment of God's favor, will be observed in this State, and the voice of Iowa will unite with the voice of her Sister States in giving thanks to the Lord for his merciful kindness. And all her citizens who recognize the favor of God in the blessings we enjoy, are requested to suspend all secular employment, and in family re-unions, social gatherings, and their accustomed places of public worship give thanks for his bountiful providence.

Thanks for the preservation of our free institutions.

Thanks that our national perils by recent events are greatly lessened, and that our people, animated by the spirit of their fathers, have resolved to maintain Liberty and Union unimpaired.

Thanks for His merciful preservation of the Ship of State amid the storm of civil strife, and invocation for its guidance into the calm waters of universal Freedom and perpetual Union.

Thanks for the numerous victories so gloriously won on Land and Sea, in the cause of freedom and humanity.

And let us devoutly pray that the God of battles will guide the heroic defenders of our Flag, and in His holy keeping shield them from danger; nor forget that their wives and little ones merit our gratitude and protection. Let us pray that continued victories may crown the efforts of our armies until treason and rebellion be crushed, and that in His own good time He will vouchsafe an honorable and permanent Peace to our Land. May our patriot soldiers sleeping in their honored graves, be remembered with the silent tear, and heartfelt prayer ascend that our patriotism be purified by their blood, and that their widows and orphans may receive Divine consolation and protection.

16

In testimony whereof, I have hereunto set my hand and caused to be affixed the Great Seal of the State of Iowa.
Done at Des Moines, this 11th day of November, A. D., 1864.

Kansas - 34th state
State Motto: "Ad Astra Per Aspera"
(To the Stars with Difficulty)

Thanksgiving Proclamation - 1862

The second year of our existence as a State is drawing to a close. The balance sheet for 1862 will soon be struck. From the earliest settlement of our country the Autumn months have been deemed most appropriate for recounting the blessings of Providence, and making public acknowledgments therefor in Thanksgiving and Praise.

As a State we have been highly favored during the year now closing. The earth has yielded abundantly, and health and general prosperity have been allotted to us. While deadly civil war has been waged on our border, and in many of the States, comparative peace and quiet have been our lot. While we mourn that civil war still spreads its desolation in our country, there is cause for thankfulness that the immutable laws of God apply as well to nations as individuals, to war as well as peace, and that there is some reason to hope that our nation is beginning to understand the application of these laws to our present condition as a people.

In view of the numberless blessings showered upon our State and Nation, I appoint, Thursday the 27th day of November next, as a day of Thanksgiving and Praise to Almighty God, and earnestly invite all good citizens to observe the same as become a Christian people: By abstaining from labor and business occupations; By attending upon public worship; By deeds of charity to the poor and needy; and by a cultivation of the domestic and social virtues.

Given under my hand and seal of the State at Topeka, this 29th day of October, 1862.

Kentucky - 15th state
State Motto: "United We Stand, Divided We Fall"

Thanksgiving Proclamation – 1860

PROCLAMATION,
BY HIS EXCELLENCY, BERIAH MAGOFFIN, GOVERNOR OF THE COMMONWEALTH OF KENTUCKY.
COMMONWEALTH OF KENTUCKY, Executive Department.

In accordance with a time-honored custom, as well as with my own convictions of propriety, I hereby designate THURSDAY, the 29th instant, as a day of public Thanksgiving and Prayer throughout the Commonwealth of Kentucky, and recommend that the people on that day abstain from their secular vocations, close their places of business, and unite in Thanksgiving to Almighty God for the countless blessings we have received at His hands, and in supplicating a continuance of His favor.

In testimony whereof, I have hereunto set my hand, and caused the seal of the Commonwealth to be affixed.

Louisiana - 18th state
State Motto: "Union, Justice, and Confidence"

Thanksgiving Proclamation - 1904

HOWEVER widely the people of this great country may differ in matters social, political and economical, there is one altar around which all may meet in fraternal communion--the altar of Almighty God, the Creator and Ruler of the Universe. The custom of annually setting apart a Day of Thanksgiving on which all may gather in their homes and places of worship and make acknowledgment to Him for his manifold blessings and benefactions to mankind constitutes not only a tribute to the omnipotence of God, but a recognition of His directing influence in tracing the destiny of the world.

During the past year Louisiana has been singularly blessed by Providence. The richest gifts of the soil have been hers; business has prospered within her borders; labor has reaped the just reward of honest toil; there has been increased production in factory and field, and her people have made gigantic strides in the march of human progress.

In all this we can distinctly trace the hand of Him who "doeth all things well." It is eminently fitting, therefore, that in addition to keeping Him "enshrined within our hearts," we should give proper public expression to our gratitude for His goodness and mercy.

In conformity with the proclamation of the President of the United States, and by virtue of the power vested in me, I, NEWTON GRAIN BLANGHARD, Governor of the State of Louisiana, do by these presents, designate Thursday, November 24, 1904, as Thanksgiving Day, and I earnestly recommend that during the whole of that day the people of Louisiana suspend, as far as is practicable, their usual business avocations, and, in their homes and houses of worship devote themselves to such services and ceremonies as will appropriately express their thanks to God for His many and gracious gifts vouchsafed us during the past year.

In Testimony Whereof, I have hereunto set my hand and caused to be affixed the Great Seal of the State of Louisiana.

Maine - 23rd state
State Motto: "Dirigo"
(I Direct)

Thanksgiving Proclamation – 1858

With the advice of the Executive Council, I appoint THURSDAY, the twenty-fifth day of November next, as a day of PUBLIC THANKSGIVING AND PRAISE.

The continual bounties and manifold mercies of a superintending and all-wise Providence, call for expressions of unfeigned gratitude and devout praise. The infinite Father, eternal Source of all good, hath crowned the year with abundance; let every heart glow with grateful love. A God of love, the Fountain of all mercies, hath averted the causes of public distress; let all unite in songs of adoration.

All nature proclaims the goodness and glory of God, maker of heaven and earth; how fit that His intelligent offspring should acknowledge Him, in Thanksgiving and Praise, as the Author of all needful blessings, and their dependence on His forbearance and loving kindness.

Especially doth it become us as a people, to join in public celebration of the Divine Goodness for the innumerable blessings vouchsafed at every period of our national existence: for succor in the struggle of our fathers for independence; for guidance in laying the foundation of free institutions; for fostering care in their infancy; for preservation amid perils internal and external, and for that paternal favor which has attended our country's progress from weakness and dependence to prosperity and power; and to render thanks, moreover, to the great Ruler of the earth, for the precious boon of civil and religious liberty, for the multiplied agencies of social and political amelioration and the means of spiritual improvement.

Given at the Council Chamber, at Augusta, this fifteenth day of October, in the year of our Lord one thousand eight hundred and fifty-eight, and of the Independence of the United States the eighty-third.

Maryland - 7ᵗʰ state
State Motto: "Fatti Maschii, Parole Femine"
(Manly Deeds, Womanly Words)

Thanksgiving Proclamation – 1904

WHEREAS, the President of the United States has by proclamation set apart Thursday, the 24th day of November, as a day of Thanksgiving and Prayer; and

Whereas The people of Maryland have great cause to be thankful for abundant harvests and for freedom from pestilence and have been blessed with peace and prosperity;

Now, therefore, I, EDWIN WARFIELD, Governor of Maryland, by virtue of authority vested in me by law, do hereby designate And proclaim Thursday, the twenty – fourth day of November instant, a Legal Holiday, and recommend its observance as a day of thanksgiving and prayer, and that the people of this Christian Commonwealth devote the day to appropriate religious services, "yielding unfeigned thanks and praise to the Giver of all good gifts to man for the return of seed time and harvest, for the increase of the ground and the gathering in of the fruits thereof, and for all other blessings of His merciful Providence bestowed upon this nation and people, and beseeching Him to continue His loving kindness to us, that our land may still yield her increase to His glory and our comfort.

In Testimony Whereof I have hereunto set my hand and caused to be affixed the Great Seal of the State of Maryland, at the Capitol, in the City of Annapolis on this 9th day of November, in the year A. D. 1904.

Massachusetts - 6ᵗʰ state
State Motto: "Ense Petit Placidam sub Libertate Quietem"
(Peace, but Peace Only Under Liberty)

Thanksgiving Proclamation – 1861

A PROCLAMATION FOR A DAY OF PUBLIC FASTING, HUMILIATION AND PRAYER.

The season has arrived when it becomes the people of Massachusetts, obediently to the pious and venerable custom of the Commonwealth, to write in the observance of their Annual Fast.

I do therefore, with the advice and consent of the Council, appoint THURSDAY, the fourth day of April next, a day of FASTING, HUMILIATION and PRAYER.

And I respectfully request the people of every persuasion, with one consent, to lay aside all unnecessary and inconsistent auctions of business and pleasure, to repair to their usual places of public worship, and to dedicate the day to earnest self-examination and to the service of God in the exercises of Devotion.

Let us penitently confess, renounce and forsake our Sins, and imploring forgiveness of the same, through the Infinite and Divine Mercy, seek for strength of purpose, purity of heart, disinterested affection and abiding faith, rightly to discern, obediently and cheerfully to observe all the duties and obligations of our future lives.

Let us recognize the Providence of the Almighty Rules of Heaven and Earth, in all the affairs of Nations and of Men.

Let us humble ourselves in the recognition of our own vanity and foolishness, whenever we have set up our own wisdom or will against His Supreme Intelligence, Love and Power.

Let us remember that the Divine requirement to do justly, and to love mercy, and to walk humbly with God, rests upon all men everywhere, and upon all nations: that there can be no national wickedness without individual guilt; no real calamity independent of human folly or misconduct, and no suffering unendurable save the misery of Remorse.

Let us carry on our hearts, before Him who is "no respecter of persons," the cause of our Country, the rights and welfare of all her people, of whatever section, race, color, or condition:

And let us be willing, in all respects, to do and to receive, and even to desire, whatever He shall deem to be the best for us, who ruleth all things well.

Given at the Council Chamber, this seventh day of March, in the year one thousand eight hundred and sixty-one, and the eighty-fifth of the Independence of the United States of America.

Michigan - 26th state
State Motto: "Si Quaeris Peninsulam Amoenam"
(If You Seek a Pleasant Peninsula, Look About You)

Thanksgiving Proclamation – 1922

"Enter into His gates with thanksgiving, and into His courts with praise: be thankful unto Him and bless His name."

WE HAVE come again to the season of the year when, in accordance with the devout custom established by our fathers more than three centuries ago, we formally set apart a day of thanksgiving and praise to Almighty God for all His mercies and blessings.

We have every reason for thankfulness. Our fields and orchards and vineyards have yielded richly of their products. Our people have been sober, industrious and steadfast. Industry and enterprise have translated the varied and unlimited resources of our commonwealth into wealth and happiness for all who have had the initiative and the capacity to do and achieve. While we face a new day big with many perplexing problems, may our faith in the integrity of American institutions be rededicated to the government which has always symbolized the best that has been achieved since the struggle for representative government began.

Therefore, by virtue of the authority vested in me as Governor of the State of Michigan, I hereby join the President of the United States in designating Thursday, November 30th, 1922, as a day of Thanksgiving and prayer.

Given under my hand and the Great Seal of the State this tenth day of November, in the year of our Lord one thousand nine

23

hundred and twenty-two, and of the Commonwealth the eighty-sixth.

Minnesota - 32nd state
State Motto: "L'etoile du Nord"
(The Star of the North)

Thanksgiving Proclamation – 1885

In obedience to law and custom I do hereby set apart and appoint Thursday, the Twenty-sixth Day of the Present Month, As a Day of Solemn and Public Thanksgiving To Almighty God, for His continued blessings and mercies.

The people of Minnesota have been led onward through another season in substantial prosperity and happiness. Peace and order have prevailed. General healthfulness has continued, and labor has obtained employment and its meed. Abundant harvests have rewarded the care of the husbandman. The violence of the elements has been tempered, and pestilence averted from the people and their flocks and herds. Our material interests have been prosecuted with success, and our hearts' concern in, and support of the great agencies of moral and social amelioration have been maintained.

Wherefore, I recommend and exhort the people of the State that on the day aforesaid, laying aside their ordinary avocations, and assembling in their usual places of worship and around their sacred firesides, they celebrate, in joyfulness of heart, with fitting words and ceremonies the praise of our Father of mercy, the Giver of every good.

Given under my hand and the Great Seal of the State, at the Capitol, in St. Paul, this Seventh day of November, A. D. One Thousand Eight Hundred and Eighty-five.

Mississippi - 20ᵗʰ state
State Motto: "Virtute et Armis"
(By Valor and Arms)

Mississippi State Constitution:

Preamble:
We, the people of Mississippi in convention assembled,
grateful to Almighty God, and invoking his blessing on our work, do
ordain and establish this constitution.

SECTION 18

...The rights hereby secured shall not be construed to justify
acts of licentiousness injurious to morals or dangerous to the peace
and safety of the state, or to exclude the Holy Bible from use in any
public school of this state.

Thanksgiving Proclamation – 1972

WHEREAS, under the provisions of Section 3-3-7, Mississippi
Code of 1972, Thanksgiving Day is declared a legal holiday in the
State of Mississippi; and
WHEREAS, during the Thanksgiving Holiday, many State
employees will travel to spend time with their families in Mississippi
and in other state; and
NOW, THEREFORE, I, Ronnie Musgrove, Governor of the State
of Mississippi, pursuant to Section 3-3-7, Mississippi Code of 1972,
hereby authorize the closing of all offices of the State of Mississippi
on Thursday, November 28, 2002, in observance of THANKSGIVING
DAY.
IN ADDITION, I hereby authorize the closing of all offices of the
State of Mississippi, in the discretion of the respective agency
heads, on Friday, November 29, 2002, in further observance of the
THANKSGIVING HOLIDAY.
IN WITNESS WHEREOF, I have hereunto set my hand and
caused the Great Seal of the State of Mississippi to be affixed.
DONE in the City of Jackson, November 4th, 2002 in the

two hundred and twenty-sixth year of the United States of America.

Missouri - 24th state
State Motto: "Salus Populi Suprema Lex Esto"
(The Welfare of the People Shall Be the Supreme Law)

Thanksgiving Proclamation – 1865

The coming month will close a year memorable in the annals of our country, and full of rich blessings, for which we should appropriately acknowledge our indebtedness to the Providence of God.

The nation has triumphed in a struggle for its existence. The oppressed have been given liberty. The hollowed scenes of peace have succeeded the horrors of civil war, and while we mourn over our dead heroes, the living ones are returned to us.

Abundant harvests have crowned the husbandman's labors; the privileges of education and the benign influences of christianity have been continued; we have been exempt from mortal plagues; prosperity has blessed the marts of commerce; we are at peace with all the world; and the future is as replete with promises as the present with blessings.

Desiring to perpetuate the good customs of our fathers, I hereby designate THURSDAY, THE SEVENTH DAY OF DECEMBER, PROXIMO, to be observed in the State of Missouri as a day of public thanksgiving and devout remembrance. I recommend that the people abondon for the day their usual avocations, and, assembling in their places of worship, engage in such religous solemnities as to them shall seem expressive of the feelings of grateful hearts; and while we thus recognize and acknowledge the goodness of God, and render thanks and praise, let us not forget to share our abundance with the widow and orphan, and him who bears decrepitude for his nation's sake.

In Testimony Whereof, I have hereunto set my hand, and caused to be affixed the Great Seal of the State, at the City of Jefferson, this fifteenth day of November, in the year of our Lord 1865, of the Independence of the United States the ninetieth, and of the State of Missouri the forty-fifth.

Montana - 41st state
State Motto: "Oro y Plata"
(Gold and Silver)

Montana State Constitution:

Preamble:
We the people of Montana grateful to God for the quiet beauty of our state, the grandeur of our mountains, the vastness of our rolling plains, and desiring to improve the quality of life, equality of opportunity and to secure the blessings of liberty for this and future generations do ordain and establish this constitution.

Nebraska - 37th state
State Motto: "Equality Before the Law"

Thanksgiving Proclamation – 1904

The element of gratitude is and should be a distinguishing trait of all enlightened people. "No man liveth to himself" and so long as there is mutual dependence so long will the human heart respond to benefits received. But there are higher duties and higher obligations then those based on temporal affairs. As a

27

people we recognize that from the Almighty proceedeth "every good and perfect gift," and it is but fitting that the deepest gratitude of which we are capable should find expression to Him both in private devotion and in public service.

The custom of setting apart a special day of thanksgiving for the mercies of the year is a fixed institution with the American people. The recurring season reminds us of bountiful harvests garnered, of general prosperity, of freedom from pestilence, of contentment and happiness around every hearthstone and of peace at home and abroad. For these and for all other blessings we are profoundly grateful.

In harmony, therefore, with the action taken by the President of the United States, I, John H. Mickey, Governor of the State of Nebraska, do hereby designate THURSDAY, NOVEMBER 24, 1904, as a day of general thanksgiving. Let the people of Nebraska carry out the true spirit of the occasion and let them assemble in their homes and in their churches, there to render the homage of grateful hearts for the manifold blessings received, and let them pledge themselves anew to the cause of righteous government and to all influences that make for a purer and better citizenship.

IN TESTIMONY WHEREOF, I have hereunto subscribed my name and caused to be affixed the Great Seal of the State.

Nevada - 36th state
State Motto: "All for Our Country"

Nevada State Constitution:

Preamble:
We the people of the State of Nevada Grateful to Almighty God for our freedom in order to secure its blessings, insure domestic tranquility, and form a more perfect Government, do establish this Constitution.

<u>Thanksgiving Proclamation – 2003</u>

One hundred and forty years ago, Abraham Lincoln, in the midst of a Civil War and great political and economic uncertainty in the country, issued the first presidential proclamation calling for "A National Thanksgiving Day." President Lincoln called upon his "fellow citizens in every part of the United States, and also those who are at sea, and those who are sojourning in foreign lands to set apart and observe the last Thursday in November next as a day of Thanksgiving and Prayer"

Lincoln also requested that the governors throughout the country issue Thanksgiving proclamations in their respective states and territories. Governor James W. Nye issued Nevada's first "Thanksgiving Proclamation" on November 17, 1863, and requested the territorial citizens to observe Thursday, November 26 as "a day of Public Thanksgiving to Almighty God for his watchfulness and protection over us as a people and as a nation through the year just passed."

Now almost 140 years later to the day, with our nation again facing challenging times, I ask my fellow Nevadans to remember the sacrifice of our forebearers, and those of us today at home and abroad, as we prepare to observe our national day of Thanksgiving on Thursday, November 27.

Now therefore I, Kenny C. Guinn, Governor for the state of Nevada, do hereby proclaim November 27, 2003, as "A Day of Thanksgiving."

New Hampshire - 9th state
State Motto: "Live Free or Die"

<u>Thanksgiving Proclamation – 1805</u>

IT has been customary for the Citizens of this State, at the recommendation of the Supreme Executive Authority, to set apart a certain day near the close of the year for the purpose of publicly recognizing their dependence upon Almighty God for protection, and that they might express their gratitude to HIM for all blessings and mercies received, and implore a continuance of them:--I therefore, in conformity to this laudable and long established practice, do by and with the advice of Council, appoint THURSDAY, the Twenty-Eighth Day of November next, to be observed as a day of PUBLIC THANKSGIVING AND PRAYER thoughout this State, hereby exhorting the People of all sects and denominations to assemble with their pastors and religious teachers, at their respective places of public worship on that day, and devote a reasonable part thereof in praising and adoring Almighty God, and in offering up our thanks to HIM as the great author of every good and perfect gift, for the many favours that he has been pleased to bestow upon us as individuals during the past year; as also for the gracious exercise of his guardian care over the great and general concerns of our common country. That although the earth has been visited by a severe and early drought, yet that by his blessing we are favoured with a competency of the fruits of the field, for the supplies of another year. That we have not been afflicted with those contagious diseases that have visited some of the Cities of our sister States, but have enjoyed a general measure of health.

That the life and health of the President of the United States have been preserved; that our civil and religious liberties are secure; and that no internal causes have occurred to disturb the peace and harmony of our Land. For the termination of our contest with one of the African powers; the liberation of our fellow-citizens from bondage, and their restoration to the arms of their country, and the sweets of liberty.--For his smiles on our Commerce, Navigation and Fisheries, and for that prosperity that has generally prevailed. But above all, for the inestimable blessing of the gospel of peace and salvation, the means of grace and hopes of future glory, through the merits of a crucified Saviour.

And while our mouths are filled with Praise and Thanksgiving, let us supplicate our Heavenly Benefactor, that he would penetrate our hearts as well with a due sense of his goodness, as of our own unworthiness, and continue to us all the blessings that we now enjoy, and bestow upon us all such additional favours as may be for our good. That he would be pleased to keep the Government of the United States under his protection; bless our Nation in all its internal and external concerns, and inspire all in authority with wisdom, and with a patriotic regard to its welfare and honour. That he would command the pestilence that now scourges some of the Cities of our country to cease its desolations, and make those Cities rejoice in the return of Health, and in the mercies of the Lord. That he would particularly keep this State under his holy and superintending care, smile upon its Agriculture, Commerce and Fisheries, and bless the labours of the labourer in every walk and department of life. That he would cherish our University, our Academies and Schools, and all other Institutions for promoting improvements in knowledge, usefulness and virtue. That he would preside in all our Courts and inspire those who make, and those who administer the Laws, with his divine wisdom; and make every branch of our civil Government subserve the best interests of the PEOPLE. That he would bless the means used for the promulgation of his word, and make pure religion and morality more and more abound. And it is hereby earnestly recommended that all persons abstain from labour and recreations unbecoming the solemnities of the day.

New Jersey - 3rd state
State Motto: "Liberty and Prosperity"

<u>Thanksgiving Proclamation – 1904</u>

Whereas, The President of these United States has appointed THURSDAY, NOVEMBER THE TWENTY-FOURTH, as a day of festival and thanksgiving by all the people of the United States, at home and abroad, for all the mercies vouchsafed to us during the past year;

Now, therefore, I, Franklin Murphy, Governor of the State of New Jersey, in accordance with a custom that has come down to us from our forefathers, do join with the President in requesting the people of this State to observe the day named as a day of thanksgiving to the Giver of all good for all His mercies to us as a people and as individuals.

I do also request that the day be observed as a day of prayer, that the blessings of an overruling Providence may be continued to us, and that we, in all humility, asking forgiveness for our sins, and for light to see the right and strength to do it, may, as far as in us lies, continue to deserve the Divine favor.

Witness my hand and the great seal of the State of New Jersey hereunto affixed. Done at the City of Trenton this fourteenth day of November, in the year of our Lord one thousand nine hundred and four, and of the Independence of the United States the one hundred and twenty-ninth.

New Mexico - 47th state
State Motto: "Crescit Eundo"
(It Grows As It Goes)

Thanksgiving Proclamation – 1902

Whereas, The time honored custom in all the United States of setting aside a day annually at this season of the year to be observed by the people especially as one of Thanksgiving for benefits and mercies shown during the past, which the President of the United States has recognized and followed by issuing his official proclamation that Thursday, the 27th day of November, A. D. 1902, be a Day of National Thanksgiving:

Now, Therefore, I, Miguel A. Otero, Governor of the Territory of New Mexico, in accordance with said custom and the Proclamation of the President, do hereby proclaim Thursday, the 27th day of November, A. D. 1902, as a Day of Public Thanksgiving and Prayer throughout the Territory of New Mexico, and earnestly urge that on that day all public and private business be suspended; that the Territorial Institutions and public schools be closed, and that the people assemble in their respective places of worship there to publicly give thanks to Almighty God for the manifold blessings granted them during the past year, for the bounteous crops and increase in material gain, as well as for their exemption from the natural disasters and human wrought evils which have afflicted some portions of our country, and to pray for a continuance of these blessings in the future. Also on that day that each of us remember the poor people and give to them of our material store in order that they may have additional cause for thanksgiving.

New York – 11th State
State Motto: "Excelsior"
(Ever Upward)

Thanksgiving Proclamation – 1900

EXECUTIVE CHAMBER
In accordance with the wise custom of our forefathers now continued for many generations, I hereby set apart Thursday, the twenty-ninth day of November, nineteen hundred, as a day of thanksgiving and prayer to the Almighty for the innumerable benefits conferred upon the citizens of this State, in common with their fellow citizens of the whole nation during the year which has just passed; for the material well being which we enjoy, and for the chances of moral betterment which are always open to us.

Done at the Capitol in the city of Albany this thirteenth day of November in the year of our Lord nineteen hundred.

North Carolina - 12th state
State Motto: "Esse Quam Videri"
(To Be Rather Than to Seem)

North Carolina State Constitution:

Preamble:
We, the people of the State of North Carolina, grateful to Almighty God, the Sovereign Ruler of Nations, for the preservation of the American Union and the existence of our civil, political and religious liberties, and acknowledging our dependence upon Him for the continuance of those blessings to us and our posterity, do, for the more certain security thereof and for the better government of this State, ordain and establish this Constitution.

Section 1. The equality and rights of persons.

We hold it to be self-evident that all persons are created equal; that they are endowed by their Creator with certain inalienable rights; that among these are life, liberty, the enjoyment of the fruits of their own labor, and the pursuit of happiness.

North Dakota - 39th state
State Motto: "Liberty and Union, Now and Forever, One and Inseparable"

Thanksgiving Proclamation – 1901

Thursday, the 28th day of November, has been designated by the President of the United States as Thanksgiving Day. This day has been set apart and made a special day all over our land to express to the Almighty Ruler our feelings of gratitude and thanks for the more than usual benefits of the past year. It has been a year of great growth in material wealth: labor in all branches has been bountifully rewarded: comfort and contentment have been with our people.

And now, at the close of the year, after the harvest has been garnered, we do well to rest from our labor and gather in our places of worship, and in our homes, and in thankfulness and joy dedicate a day to grateful acknowledgment of the Divine Providence which has been over us for the past year: I do, therefore, appoint Thursday, the Twenty-eighth Day of November, Thanksgiving Day for the State of North Dakota.

Given under my hand and the Great Seal of the State, at the Capitol in Bismarck, this 11th day of November, A. D. 1901.

Ohio - 17th state
State Motto: "With God, All Things Are Possible"

Thanksgiving Proclamation – 1865

Yet another year has passed over our State, and Nation! And the people of Ohio, in accordance with a usage of our dead fathers, older than the State itself, have been once again invoked, by a joint resolution of their General Assembly, to unite in a public acknowledgment, as well of the existence, power, and goodness of God, as of His interposing hand in all the works, ways and relations of men.

And, now, upon a full consideration of all the religious truths connected with this venerable custom, and with a lively remembrance of all the events of that past year, what ought this whole people to feel and to utter, at their family re-unions, in the greetings of friends and neighbors, and around the altars of the Most High? Can it be possible, that any people ever before could have had such causes as ourselves, for thankfulness and praises to God? If the annually recurring seasons of the regular year and the

35

varying climates of our globe, with all their goodly fruits and health and other countless comforts and delights, have ever been and shall always be, severally and in their due succession, fittest causes for grateful homage to that benign Heart and bounteous Hand, from which they ever flow, what can we feel,--what shall we say,-- of our debt of gratitude for His works and mercies in this, the most memorable of all the years? All those natural and general blessings we have fully shared with others. But, a great nation, desperately imperiled, has been grandly saved. And that nation was--is--ours! Surely, surely, if ever a State and Nation in all history, had more than fittest and fullest cause to give thanks unto the Lord for His wondrous benefits and forbearances, very surely are they these of ours, here and now! For, whereas, at our former festivals, we were at war, we are now in peace; we were divided, we are one; we were poor and weak, we are rich and strong; we were pitied, or despised, by all the nations of the earth, and are we not envied and honored among and above them all? Then, Slavery, like a vast pall of night-shade, blackened our whole bright sky and degraded and disgraced all our fair land. Now, Liberty, like a new risen sun, with healing in his beams, shines and glows, under all our heavens, upon our whole earth and into every American mind and heart. Wondrous, happy, glorious, change! Well may we sing in the words of that singer after God's own heart, amongst his former chosen people: "Thou hast turned, for me, my mourning into dancing; thou hast put off my sackcloth, and girded me with gladness."

Let us then, fellow-citizens, each and all--all and each one of us--"Give thanks unto the Lord, for He is good; for His mercy endureth forever;" "It is a good thing to give thanks unto the Lord, and to sing praises to His name." Nor, (let casuists and doubters deny as they may), shall these, our songs, be a vain thing; for, if we may not, by our prayers and praises, bend the Divine will and love to us, surely we can raise ours towards Him.

Now, therefore, I, Charles Anderson, Governor of the State of Ohio, do hereby appoint the last Thursday, being the 30th day of the present month of November, as a day of general Thanksgiving and Praise to that God of Love, who has so loved and blessed this land and people. And I do, furthermore, most respectfully, but earnestly, request all the people of this State, who love their country and their God, upon that day to lay aside all their customary cares and vocations; to gather their scattered children around the brightened hearths and the cheerful boards of their olden family homes; to render thanks there, and in the public temples, to the Heavenly Father, for all his past benefits, and, especially, for His amazing and glorious works of the past year; to implore a continuance and increase of them, and most especially, of that highest and best of all temporal blessings-- Peace and Good Will amongst men; and, finally, that in the true spirit of that cheerful, Christian thankfulness to God, and of good will towards men, which is suitable to an occasion so extraordinary, we shall, for ourselves, strive, henceforth, so to live with our fellow- citizens and our fellow-men, everywhere throughout our now redeemed and reunited land, as to prove ourselves worthy to be the common citizens of such a country, and the common children of such a God.

In Testimony Whereof, I have hereunto set my name and caused the Great Seal of the State of Ohio to be affixed, at Columbus, on this, the third day of November, in the year of our Lord one thousand eight hundred and sixty-five, and in the ninetieth year of the Independence of the United States of America.

Oklahoma - 46th state
State Motto: "Labor Omnia Vincit"
(Labor Conquers All Things)

Thanksgiving Proclamation – 1902

Providence has bestowed upon the citizens of Oklahoma many blessings during the year which is now drawing to a close. Our fields have brought forth plentifully and our harvests have been abundant.

All legitimate lines of commerce in our Territory have brought good results. The golden sunlight of Prosperity has fallen upon all alike.

Citizens of our beloved commonwealth have much to be proud of and much to be thankful for, and it is with one accord that the people hail with joyful anticipation that day in the not distant future when a change shall be wrought upon the banner of our great republic, and when upon that field of blue shall be seen another star, and that star shall represent our own beautiful Oklahoma, sun kissed "Land of The Fair God."

In conformity with established custom and in harmony with the proclamation of the President of the United States, I recommend that Thursday, November 27th, 1902, be observed as a day set apart for devotion and thanksgiving, and in this manner manifest our gratitude to the Author of all good gifts for the moral, intellectual and material blessings so lavishly bestowed during the past, and for the rich promise and glorious prophesy of the future.

Oregon - 33rd state
State Motto: "She Flies with Her Own Wings"

Thanksgiving Proclamation – 1903

The President of the United States of America has designated Thursday, the twenty-sixth day of November, A. D. 1903, as a day of general thanksgiving, and conformable to a time-honored custom and in accordance with the Proclamation of the President, I, Geo. E. Chamberlain, Governor of the State of Oregon, do hereby set apart said day as a holiday, and do recommend that in so far as possible all business be suspended so that the people may avail themselves of an opportunity thus afforded to rest from their labors and to return to Almighty God, Giver of every good and perfect gift, grateful thanks for the manifold blessings they enjoy.

In Witness Whereof, I have hereunto set my hand and caused the Great Seal of State to be hereunto affixed at the City of Salem, this twelfth day of November, in the year of our Lord one thousand nine hundred and three.

Pennsylvania - 2nd state
State Motto: "Virtue, Liberty, and Independence"

Thanksgiving Proclamation – 1918

THE blessings of Almighty God fill and overflow the measure of our joy. The Harpies will prey upon civilization no more. Once again we may sit under our own vine and fig tree at peace and unafraid. The fateful fallacies of might have again been revealed. Right is enthroned among nations. The higher, holier laws of love and justice are reestablished. The flags of battle are furled.
"THE EPOCH ENDS, THE WORLD IS STILL."
For this many other blessings vouchsafed us we have, more than ever before in the life of our Country and Commonwealth, occasion for profound Thankfulness. While we have won an honorable victory let it never be forgotten that only those nations are blessed whose God is the Lord. Unless we become a chastened and increasingly devout people our victory on the battle front will prove our ultimate defeat. We have been inordinately wasteful and careless. We have never learned the vital lessons of thrift and conservation. We have wasted enough to feed and clothe all our own unfortunates and to give generously to all suffering and dependent people throughout the world. Let us take thought of all our national faults and before God solemnly confess our wrongs and pledge ourselves to be a more sane, a more devout, a more unselfish, a more consecrated people than we have ever been before.
We are offering our form of government and the blessings it has given us to the oppressed peoples of many lands. Let us see to it that the democracy we offer is clean and wholesome throughout. Let us give to them only the best our refinements of life and character can formulate. Let us remove from our government every ill, from our people every wrong, that we may offer only the

ideally splendid to others.

Soon our boys will come marching home in honor and in victory. How glad will be our welcome! With bands and banners, with tears and cheers, we shall welcome them home. Let us not forget the heroic sons of Pennsylvania who will not come marching home. They have given the full measure of devotion to our country and to civilization. Let us not forget the superb sacrifice of the women of this Commonwealth who with fine spirit of service gave them parting blessing, who would gladly give them heartiest welcome. They now sit in silent sorrow by lonely hearth stones. Surely for our brave boys, for their wives and mothers we shall accept the issues of this world war in solemn joy in deep humility. Let our people humble themselves before God and be glad to do His will.

When the Christ of the world was born the angels sang "Glory to God in the highest, peace on earth; good will to men." In the same reverent and holy spirit I hereby designate and appoint THURSDAY, NOVEMBER 28, 1918 AS THANKSGIVING DAY and call upon our people on that day to lay aside all accustomed duties and quietly gather with one accord in our places of worship to give thanks that He has given us a year of chastening and a day of peace. Let us be glad also that with the ending of the war has come an end to the frightful malady that has wrought unprecedented loss of life in this Commonwealth. Let us on that day manifest the true quality of our faith in God. Let us count our blessings. Let us consider our ways. Let us resolve to walk steadily and humbly in His steps. Let us thank Him for the coming of our Lord and for the principles of love and peace He has set for men. Let us so plan and so live that we may manifest to all the sacred security of individuals and of nations when they do righteously and sin not.

GIVEN under my hand and the Great Seal of the State, at the City of Harrisburg, this nineteenth day of November in the year of our Lord one thousand nine hundred and eighteen and of the Commonwealth the one hundred and forty-third.

Rhode Island - 13th state
State Motto: "Hope"

Thanksgiving Proclamation – 1842

WHEREAS the General Assembly of the State aforesaid, on the fifth day of November instant, passed the following Resolutions, to wit:

Resolved, That Thursday, the twenty-fourth day of November instant, be set apart as a day of Public Thanksgiving and Praise to Almighty God; and that it be recommended to the people of Rhode-Island, abstaining, on that day, from all unnecessary labor and unbecoming recreation, to assemble in their places of public worship, and to render unto the Father of their spirits, and the Giver of all their blessings, the tribute of devout and grateful heart; to thank Him for the services which He hath vouchsafed to us during the year which has passed; for the goodness which hath crowned the year with plenty, and for the mercy which has averted the pestilence that walketh in darkness: for His gracious care of the welfare of our common country, in preserving to her the blessings of peace with other nations, and of permitting her to enjoy, under the operation of equal and popular systems of government, the varied social happiness which springs from freedom, regulated by law. And as a people to whom has been bequeathed by venerated ancestors, a rich legacy of civil and religious liberty, to acknowledge, with fervent gratitude, that the lines are fallen to us in pleasant places--that we have, indeed, a goodly heritage--for here was put forth the first great experiment of complete freedom in religious concernments--here was struck the first blow in the revolutionary contest with Great Britain, and here has been maintained, and triumphantly maintained, by the unaided vigor of our people, the first controversy, since the adoption of the American Constitution, with the spirit of licentiousness and anarchy. Chastended by the trials through which we have been called to pass, and remembering the mercy which hath delivered us from peril, it becometh us as a people, to lift up the voice of thanksgiving and praise to Him who so graciously interposed to help and to save us; and especially doth it become us, knowing that unless the Lord keep the City, the watchman waketh but in vain, to invoke him to continue his watchful care over us, and to plant in all hearts the spirit of social concord, a deeper love for the imperishable principles of temperate freedom, a truer reverence for the wisdom of the Just. While invoking the blessings of Almighty God upon all the social interests and ties with which we have to do, let us beseech Him to forgive us all our sins, negligences and ignorances, and through faith in Jesus Christ, to grant us in this world knowledge of his truth, and in the world to come life everlasting.

Resolved also, That his Excellency the Governor, be requested to issue his Proclamation, to make known the foregoing resolutions to the good people of this State.

I do therefore, pursuant to the above recited Resolution, issue this my Proclamation, to make known the same, that the good people of this State may conform thereto.

Given under my hand and the Seal of said State, at Providence, this seventh day of November, in the year of our Lord one thousand eight hundred and forty-two, and of Independence the sixty-seventh.

South Carolina - 8th state
State Motto: "Sum Spiro Spero"
(While I Breathe, I Hope)

South Carolina State Constitution:

Preamble:
We, the people of the State of South Carolina, in Convention assembled, grateful to God for our liberties, do ordain and establish this Constitution for the preservation and perpetuation of the same.

ARTICLE VI.
OFFICERS
SECTION 2

No person who denies the existence of the Supreme Being shall hold any office under this Constitution.

SECTION 4

The Governor, Lieutenant Governor, and all other officers of the State and its political subdivisions, before entering upon the duties of their respective offices, shall take and subscribe the oath of office as prescribed in section 5 of this article.

SECTION 5

Members of the General Assembly, and all officers, before they enter upon the duties of their respective offices, and all members of the bar, before they enter upon the practice of their profession, shall take and subscribe the following oath: "I do solemnly swear (or affirm) that I am duly qualified, according to the Constitution of this State, to exercise the duties of the office to which I have been elected, (or appointed), and that I will, to the best of my ability, discharge the duties thereof, and preserve, protect, and defend the Constitution of this State and of the United States. So help me God."

South Dakota - 40th state
State Motto: "Under God, the People Rule"

Thanksgiving Proclamation – 1904

The closing year has been replete with evidences of divine goodness. The prevalence of health, our bountiful harvests, the marvelous increasing prosperity, the stability of peace and

43

order, and the continued enjoyment of civil and religious liberty--
these and countless other blessings are cause for reverent
thanksgiving and rejoicing.

In the presence of the mystery of life and death, man
reverently feels his dependence upon Almighty God. Our State
and Nation recognize the hand of Providence in human affairs. In
the midst of unparalleled development, wrestling with the great
problems of a complex civilization, it is meet and proper that the
people of our commonwealth should pause and observe a
special holiday of thanksgiving and prayer.

Now, therefore, in recognition of a sacred custom and in
conformity with the proclamation of the President, I, Charles N.
Herreid, Governor of the State of South Dakota, do hereby
designate Thursday, the 24th Day of November In the year of our
Lord nineteen hundred and four, as a day of Thanksgiving to God
for the bounties of His providence and in acknowledgment of His
goodness, mercy and power, invoke his continued care and
protection. On that day let our people cease from their
accustomed occupations and in their homes and places of public
worship, with heart and voice, acknowledge the innumerable
blessings which have fallen upon us.

IN TESTIMONY WHEREOF, I have hereunto set my hand and
caused to be affixed the Great Seal of the State.

Tennessee - 16th state
State Motto: "Agriculture and Commerce"

Thanksgiving Proclamation – 1903

A WISE custom ordains that we, a christian people, shall
annually set apart one day to make fitting acknowledgement to
Almighty God for the manifold blessings vouch-safed to us as a
nation.

In no State of the Union is there more cause for grateful
thanksgiving than in Tennessee. Here we have enjoyed the liberty

and security guaranteed by a peaceful and orderly government; we have marvelously grown and prospered as a State and people; our fields have yielded an abundant harvest; our mines and factories and varied industries have responded in rich abundance to the hand of labor. We have been spared the affliction of plague and pestilence; Providence has bountifully blessed us as a people with peace with all mankind, and plenty without stint.

THEREFORE, I, JAMES B. FRAZIER, Governor of the State of Tennessee, do hereby designate Thursday, November 26th, 1903, as a day of Thanksgiving, and do earnestly recommend that all the people of this Commonwealth, on that day, cease from their ordinary avocations and assemble in their respective houses of worship, and there give thanks to God for his many and gracious gifts to us as a people.

IN TESTIMONY WHEREOF, I have hereunto set my hand, and caused the Great Seal of the State to be affixed at the Capitol, in Nashville, this the 6th day of November, 1903.

Texas - 28th state
State Motto: "Friendship"

Texas State Constitution:

Preamble:
Humbly invoking the blessings of Almighty God, the people of the State of Texas, do ordain and establish this Constitution.

Article 1 - BILL OF RIGHTS
Section 4 - RELIGIOUS TESTS

No religious test shall ever be required as a qualification to any office, or public trust, in this State; nor shall any one be excluded from holding office on account of his religious sentiments, provided he acknowledge the existence of a Supreme Being.

Utah - 45ᵗʰ state
State Motto: "Industry"

Thanksgiving Proclamation – 1883

THE custom of setting apart one day in the year to be devoted to Thanksgiving and Praise has come down to us from the Colonial Period of our history. In those early times the pilgrim founders of New England, established the custom which has become national in its observance, of returning thanks after the gathering of the crops, to the Lord of the Harvest.

I, therefore, in accordance with the Proclamation by the President, respectfully recommend that Thursday, the 29th day of November, be observed by the people of this Territory, as a day of "Thanksgiving and Praise," for the great prosperity which has marked the year now drawing to a close, and that the more wealthy remember the poor and the needy.

In Testimony Whereof, I have hereunto set my hand and caused the Great Seal of the Territory to be affixed.

Vermont - 14ᵗʰ state
State Motto: "Freedom and Unity"

Thanksgiving proclamation – 1904

"We have heard with our ears, O God. Our fathers have told us what Thou didst in their day, in the times of old."

"Offer unto God Thanksgiving; and pay thy vows unto the

Most High."

Our fathers, after their days of privation and distress, showed an exalted faith in the principles for which they fought, by setting aside a day of Thanksgiving and Prayer to God for His multiplied mercies to them.

After years of prosperity and plenty, let us not be unmindful of the same mercies, nor forget to return thanks to Almighty God for all His benefits.

In accordance with this custom, and in compliance with the proclamation of the President, I do hereby appoint Thursday, November 24, 1904, Thanksgiving Day, for the people of the State of Vermont.

On that day, in the spirit of a broader charity, let us bring good cheer to those less fortunate than ourselves; around the festive board and the glowing hearthstone, let us bind closer the ties of kindred and friendship, and in our accustomed places of worship and at the family altar, let us render thanks to God for His abundant blessings to us as individuals, as a State, and as a Nation, at peace with ourselves and the world.

Given under my hand and the Seal of the State, in the Executive Chamber at Montpelier, this Twelfth day of November, in the year of our Lord, one thousand nine hundred and four, and of the Independence of the United States the one hundred and twenty-ninth.

Virginia - 10th state
State Motto: "Sic Semper Tyrannis"
(Thus Always to Tyrants)

Thanksgiving Proclamation – 1910

Whereas, the people of this Commonwealth have during the past year enjoyed to a marked degree the blessings of God in abundant harvests, good health, happy homes, and great progress and advancement in all directions, it is especially fitting that, following the suggestion of the President of the United States, we should set apart a day for the manifestation of our gratitude:

Therefore, I, William Hodges Mann, Governor of Virginia, do fix upon Thursday, the 24th Day of November as a day of thanksgiving and prayer to the Giver of all good, and enjoin upon the citizens of this Commonwealth to assemble in their places of worship, and to the members of families to meet together in their homes to offer up grateful prayers and thanksgiving, and to ask God, as the Father of His people, to bless our homes and firesides, and make us a people whose God is the Lord.

Given under my hand and under the Lesser Seal of the Commonweath, at Richmond, this ninth day of November, in the year of our Lord one thousand nine hundred and ten, and in the one hundred and thirty-fifth year of the Commonwealth.

Washington - 42nd state
State Motto: "Alki"
(Bye and Bye)

Washington State Constitution:

Preamble:
We, the people of the State of Washington, grateful to the Supreme Ruler of the Universe for our liberties, do ordain this constitution.

West Virginia - 35th state
State Motto: "Montani Semper Liberi"
(Mountaineers Are Always Free)

Thanksgiving Proclamation - 1885

In conformity with the custom and sentiment of our people, and in accordance with the recommendation of the President of the United States, I hereby designate Thursday, the 26th Day of November, instant, as a day of Public Thanksgiving and Praise.

And I do recommend that, upon that day, all secular business be suspended and that the people, assembling at their usual places of worship, in humble recognition of human dependance upon Divine will, give all honor and glory to the Most High, for the unmerited blessings and mercies that have continued the peace, prosperity and liberty of our whole land. And remembering in prayer, the suffering poor, may they be aided and comforted by hearts of sympathy and bountiful hands.

IN TESTIMONY WHEREOF, I have hereunto set my hand and caused to be affixed the less seal of the State, at Charleston, this 16th day of November in the year of our Lord, one thousand eight hundred and eighty five, and of the State the twenty-third.

Wisconsin - 30th state
State Motto: "Forward"

Thanksgiving Proclamation – 1900

A Year of unequaled prosperity in all branches of industry, without disaster in any form, gives reason for a feeling of gratitude on the part of the people.

To give opportunity for a public expression of this feeling, and in conformity with the law of the State and a proclamation by the President of the United State, I, Edward Scofield, Governor of the State of Wisconsin, do hereby designate and set apart Thursday, November 29, 1900, to be a day of public thanksgiving.

I recommend that upon that day the people of the State, laying aside their usual occupations and industries, and assembling in their places of worship and around the family board, do express in fitting manner their gratitude to Almighty God for the blessings which have fallen upon our State and nation. New responsibilities of profound import have come upon us as a nation, and it should inspire in us a feeling of thankfulness that we are possessed of the moral and material resources necessary to meet them. A people without gratitude are unworthy of prosperity, while they who cultivate a spirit of gratitude are fitted thereby to more wisely meet responsibilites and use the blessings which come to them.

In Testimony Whereof, I have hereunto set my hand and caused the Great Seal of the State of Wisconsin to be affixed.

Wyoming - 44th state
State Motto: "Equal Rights"

NATIONAL DAY OF PRAYER – 2000

PRAYER plays a vital role in the lives of individual Americans and in the life of the nation as a whole. Historically our state and national leaders have turned to prayer in times of crisis, as well as during times of peace, prosperity, and thanksgiving.

THE CONTINENTAL CONGRESS that declared our independence also proclaimed a National Day of Prayer. President Lincoln sought to preserve our torn nation by declaring a day of prayer.

THE UNITED STATES CONGRESS passed Joint Resolution 382 on April 17, 1952 establishing an annual National Day of Prayer to join us together as a nation. President Truman signed into law PL 324, the observance of an annual National Day of Prayer.

PRESIDENT REAGAN permanently established the first Thursday of May to be the National Day of Prayer when he signed PL 100-307.

THE THEME for the 2000 National Day of Prayer is "PRAY2K, America's Hope for the New Millennium." Last year, there were more than 20,000 public gatherings nationwide. This year, over 2.5 million people are expected to gather across our great land to observe the 49th annual National Day of Prayer.

FOR THESE SIGNIFICANT REASONS, I, JIM GERINGER, Governor of the State of Wyoming, do hereby proclaim May 4th, 2000, to be a commemoration of the "NATIONAL DAY OF PRAYER" in Wyoming, and call upon the citizens of Wyoming to join with me in prayer, giving thanks to God and seeking His continued guidance and strength.

IN WITNESS WHEREOF, I have hereunto set my hand and caused the Great Seal of the State of Wyoming to be affixed this 29th day of March, 2000.

Presidential Recognition of God

In our government's history, there have been 42 US Presidents (1 holding office twice) of many different political parties: 2 Federalists, 4 Democrat-Republicans, 4 Whigs, 1 Union party, 13 Democrats, and 18 Republicans. Their political philosophies stretched from morally conservative to socially liberal to apolitically economic. Campaigns grew fierce and dirty over time, each side accusing each other of representing ultimate evil. However, each of these Presidents - every one of them - officially acknowledged God in the life of the nation, many calling on the people to intercede to this Governing Being to care for the nation and to ensure national success.

I have included the denominations of each of the Presidents for informational purposes.

As with the states, many Presidents spoke of God often. However, for space and form, I have tried to limit the Presidential quotes to one or two sources. However, there are as many Presidential quotes not given as are provided.

As you follow the quotes from each President, you will see the personal importance that each gave their faith and will see a continuous, two-century-long tradition of faithfully and officially acknowledging God.

George Washington - 1st President (1789-1797)
Political Party: Federalist
Denomination: Episcopalian

<u>Inaugural Address – 1789</u>

Such being the impressions under which I have, in obedience to the public summons, repaired to the present station, it would be peculiarly improper to omit in this first official act my fervent supplications to that Almighty Being who rules over the universe, who presides in the councils of nations, and whose providential aids can supply every human defect, that His benediction may consecrate to the liberties and happiness of the people of the United States a Government instituted by themselves for these essential purposes, and may enable every instrument employed in its administration to execute with success the functions allotted to his charge. In tendering this homage to the Great Author of every public and private good, I assure myself that it expresses your sentiments not less than my own, nor those of my fellow- citizens at large less than either. No people can be bound to acknowledge and adore the Invisible Hand which conducts the affairs of men more than those of the United States. Every step by which they have advanced to the character of an independent nation seems to have been distinguished by some token of providential agency; and in the important revolution just accomplished in the system of their united government the tranquil deliberations and voluntary consent of so many distinct communities from which the event has resulted can not be compared with the means by which most governments have been established without some return of pious gratitude, along with an humble anticipation of the future blessings which the past seem to presage.

I dwell on this prospect with every satisfaction which an ardent love for my country can inspire, since there is no truth more thoroughly established than that there exists in the economy and course of nature an indissoluble union between virtue and happiness; between duty and advantage; between the genuine maxims of an honest and magnanimous policy and the solid rewards of public prosperity and felicity; since we ought to be no less persuaded that the propitious smiles of Heaven can never be expected on a nation that disregards the eternal rules of order and right which Heaven itself has ordained

Having thus imparted to you my sentiments as they have been awakened by the occasion which brings us together, I shall take my present leave; but not without resorting once more to the benign Parent of the Human Race in humble supplication that, since He has been pleased to favor the American people with opportunities for deliberating in perfect tranquillity, and dispositions for deciding with unparalleled unanimity on a form of government for the security of their union and the advancement of their happiness, so His divine blessing may be equally conspicuous in the enlarged views, the temperate consultations, and the wise measures on which the success of this Government must depend.

John Adams – 2nd President (1797-1801)
Political Party: Federalist
Denomination: Unitarian

Inaugural Address –1797

...with humble reverence, I feel it to be my duty to add, if a veneration for the religion of a people who profess and call themselves Christians, and a fixed resolution to consider a decent respect for Christianity among the best recommendations for the public service, can enable me in any degree to comply with your wishes, it shall be my strenuous endeavor that this sagacious injunction of the two Houses shall not be without effect.

With this great example before me, with the sense and spirit, the faith and honor, the duty and interest, of the same American people pledged to support the Constitution of the United States, I entertain no doubt of its continuance in all its energy, and my mind is prepared without hesitation to lay myself under the most solemn obligations to support it to the utmost of my power.

And may that Being who is supreme over all, the Patron of Order, the Fountain of Justice, and the Protector in all ages of the world of virtuous liberty, continue His blessing upon this nation and its Government and give it all possible success and duration consistent with the ends of His providence.

Thomas Jefferson – 3rd President (1801-1809)
Political Party: Democrat-Republican
Denomination: No Specific Denomination

Inaugural Address – 1801

...enlightened by a benign religion, professed, indeed, and practiced in various forms, yet all of them inculcating honesty, truth, temperance, gratitude, and the love of man; acknowledging and adoring an overruling Providence, which by all its dispensations proves that it delights in the happiness of man here and his greater happiness hereafter... And may that Infinite Power which rules the destinies of the universe lead our councils to what is best, and give them a favorable issue for your peace and prosperity.

Letter to the Danbury Baptist Association - 1802

I reciprocate your kind prayers for the protection & blessing of the common father and creator of man, and tender you for yourselves & your religious association, assurances of my high respect & esteem.

James Madison – 4th President (1809-1817)
Political Party: Democrat-Republican
Denomination: Episcopalian

<u>Inaugural Address – 1809</u>

But the source to which I look or the aids which alone can supply my deficiencies is in the well-tried intelligence and virtue of my fellow-citizens, and in the counsels of those representing them in the other departments associated in the care of the national interests. In these my confidence will under every difficulty be best placed, next to that which we have all been encouraged to feel in the guardianship and guidance of that Almighty Being whose power regulates the destiny of nations, whose blessings have been so conspicuously dispensed to this rising Republic, and to whom we are bound to address our devout gratitude for the past, as well as our fervent supplications and best hopes for the future.

James Monroe – 5th President (1817-1825)
Political Party: Democrat-Republican
Denomination: Episcopalian

<u>Second Inaugural Address – 1821</u>

In surmounting, in favor of my humble pretensions, the difficulties which so often produce division in like occurrences, it is obvious that other powerful causes, indicating the great strength and stability of our Union, have essentially contributed to draw you together. That these powerful causes exist, and that they are permanent, is my fixed opinion; that they may produce a like accord in all questions touching, however remotely, the liberty, prosperity, and happiness of our country will always be the object of my most fervent prayers to the Supreme Author of All Good.

…With full confidence in the continuance of that candor and generous indulgence from my fellow-citizens at large which I have heretofore experienced, and with a firm reliance on the protection of Almighty God, I shall forthwith commence the duties of the high trust to which you have called me.

John Quincy Adams – 6th President (1825-1829)
Political Party: Democrat-Republican
Denomination: Unitarian

Inaugural Address – 1825

In compliance with an usage coeval with the existence of our Federal Constitution, and sanctioned by the example of my predecessors in the career upon which I am about to enter, I appear, my fellow-citizens, in your presence and in that of Heaven to bind myself by the solemnities of religious obligation to the faithful performance of the duties allotted to me in the station to which I have been called.

To the guidance of the legislative councils, to the assistance of the executive and subordinate departments, to the friendly cooperation of the respective State governments, to the candid and liberal support of the people so far as it may be deserved by honest industry and zeal, I shall look for whatever success may attend my public service; and knowing that "except the Lord keep the city the watchman waketh but in vain," with fervent supplications for His favor, to His overruling providence I commit with humble but fearless confidence my own fate and the future destinies of my country.

Andrew Jackson – 7th President (1829-1837)
Political Party: Democrat
Denomination: Presbyterian

<u>Second Inaugural Address – 1833</u>

Finally, it is my most fervent prayer to that Almighty Being before whom I now stand, and who has kept us in His hands from the infancy of our Republic to the present day, that He will so overrule all my intentions and actions and inspire the hearts of my fellow-citizens that we may be preserved from dangers of all kinds and continue forever a united and happy people.

Martin Van Buren – 8th President (1837-1841)
Political Party: Democrat
Denomination: Dutch Reformed

<u>Inaugural Address – 1837</u>

So sensibly, fellow-citizens, do these circumstances press themselves upon me that I should not dare to enter upon my path of duty did I not look for the generous aid of those who will be associated with me in the various and coordinate branches of the Government; did I not repose with unwavering reliance on the patriotism, the intelligence, and the kindness of a people who never yet deserted a public servant honestly laboring their cause; and, above all, did I not permit myself humbly to hope for the sustaining support of an ever-watchful and beneficent Providence.

Beyond that I only look to the gracious protection of the Divine Being whose strengthening support I humbly solicit, and whom I fervently pray to look down upon us all. May it be among the dispensations of His providence to bless our beloved country with honors and with length of days. May her ways be ways of pleasantness and all her paths be peace!

William Henry Harrison – 9th President (1841-1841)
Political Party: Whig
Denomination: Episcopalian

Inaugural Address – 1841

However strong may be my present purpose to realize the expectations of a magnanimous and confiding people, I too well understand the dangerous temptations to which I shall be exposed from the magnitude of the power which it has been the pleasure of the people to commit to my hands not to place my chief confidence upon the aid of that Almighty Power which has hitherto protected me and enabled me to bring to favorable issues other important but still greatly inferior trusts heretofore confided to me by my country.

We admit of no government by divine right, believing that so far as power is concerned the Beneficent Creator has made no distinction amongst men; that all are upon an equality, and that the only legitimate right to govern is an express grant of power from the governed.

These precious privileges, and those scarcely less important of giving expression to his thoughts and opinions, either by writing or speaking, unrestrained but by the liability for injury to others, and that of a full participation in all the advantages which flow from the Government, the acknowledged property of all, the American citizen derives from no charter granted by his fellow-man. He claims them because he is himself a man, fashioned by the same Almighty hand as the rest of his species and entitled to a full share of the blessings with which He has endowed them.

...I deem the present occasion sufficiently important and solemn to justify me in expressing to my fellow-citizens a profound reverence for the Christian religion and a thorough conviction that sound morals, religious liberty, and a just sense of religious responsibility are essentially connected with all true and lasting happiness; and to that good Being who has blessed us by the gifts of civil and religious freedom, who watched over and prospered the labors of our fathers and has hither to preserved to us institutions far exceeding in excellence those of any other people, let us unite in fervently commending every interest of our beloved country in all future time.

John Tyler – 10th President (1841-1845)
Political Party: Whig
Denomination: Episcopalian

3rd Annual Message – 1843

If any people ever had cause to render up thanks to the Supreme Being for parental care and protection extended to them in all the trials and difficulties to which they have been from time to time exposed, we certainly are that people. From the first settlement of our forefathers on this continent, through the dangers attendant upon the occupation of a savage wilderness, through a long period of colonial dependence, through the War of the Revolution, in the wisdom which led to the adoption of the existing forms of republican government, in the hazards incident to a war subsequently waged with one of the most powerful nations of the earth, in the increase of our population, in the spread of the arts and sciences, and in the strength and durability conferred on political institutions emanating from the people and sustained by their will, the superintendence of an overruling Providence has been plainly visible. As preparatory, therefore, to entering once more upon the high duties of legislation, it becomes us humbly to acknowledge our dependence upon Him as our guide and protector and to implore a continuance of His parental watchfulness over our beloved country. We have new cause for the expression of our gratitude in the preservation of the health of our fellow-citizens, with some partial and local exceptions, during the past season, for the abundance with which the earth has yielded up its fruits to the labors of the husbandman, for the renewed activity which has been imparted to commerce, for the revival of trade in all its departments, for the increased rewards attendant on the exercise of the mechanic arts, for the continued growth of our population and the rapidly reviving prosperity of the whole country.

I shall be permitted to congratulate the country that under an overruling Providence peace was preserved without a sacrifice of the national honor; the war in Florida was brought to a speedy termination; a large portion of the claims on Mexico have been fully adjudicated and are in a course of payment, while justice has been rendered to us in other matters by other nations; confidence between man and man is in a great measure restored and the credit of this Government fully and perfectly reestablished; commerce is becoming more and more extended in its operations and manufacturing and mechanical industry once more reap the rewards of skill and labor honestly applied; the operations of trade rest on a sound currency and the rates of exchange are reduced to their lowest amount.

James K Polk – 11th President (1845-1849)
Political Party: Democrat
Denomination: Presbyterian/ Methodist

Inaugural Address – 1845

In assuming responsibilities so vast I fervently invoke the aid of that Almighty Ruler of the Universe in whose hands are the destinies of nations and of men to guard this Heaven-favored land against the mischiefs which without His guidance might arise from an unwise public policy. With a firm reliance upon the wisdom of Omnipotence to sustain and direct me in the path of duty which I am appointed to pursue, I stand in the presence of this assembled multitude of my countrymen to take upon myself the solemn obligation "to the best of my ability to preserve, protect, and defend the Constitution of the United States."

Confidently relying upon the aid and assistance of the coordinate departments of the Government in conducting our public affairs, I enter upon the discharge of the high duties which have been assigned me by the people, again humbly supplicating that Divine Being who has watched over and protected our beloved country from its infancy to the present hour to continue His gracious benedictions upon us, that we may continue to be a prosperous and happy people.

Zachary Taylor – 12th President (1849-1850)
Political Party: Whig
Denomination: Episcopalian

<u>Inaugural Address – 1849</u>

In conclusion I congratulate you, my fellow-citizens, upon the high state of prosperity to which the goodness of Divine Providence has conducted our common country. Let us invoke a continuance of the same protecting care which has led us from small beginnings to the eminence we this day occupy, and let us seek to deserve that continuance by prudence and moderation in our councils, by well-directed attempts to assuage the bitterness which too often marks unavoidable differences of opinion, by the promulgation and practice of just and liberal principles, and by an enlarged patriotism, which shall acknowledge no limits but those of our own widespread Republic.

Millard Fillmore – 13th President (1850-1853)
Political Party: Whig
Denomination: Unitarian

1st Annual Message – 1850

And now, fellow-citizens, I can not bring this communication to a close without invoking you to join me in humble and devout thanks to the Great Ruler of Nations for the multiplied blessings which He has graciously bestowed upon us. His hand, so often visible in our preservation, has stayed the pestilence, saved us from foreign wars and domestic disturbances, and scattered plenty throughout the land. Our liberties, religions and civil, have been maintained, the fountains of knowledge have all been kept open, and means of happiness widely spread and generally enjoyed greater than have fallen to the lot of any other nation. And while deeply penetrated with gratitude for the past, let us hope that His all-wise providence will so guide our counsels as that they shall result in giving satisfaction to our constituents, securing the peace of the country, and adding new strength to the united Government under which we live.

Franklin Pierce – 14th President (1853-1857)
Political Party: Democrat
Denomination: Episcopalian

Inaugural Address – 1853

…The energy with which that great conflict was opened and, under the guidance of a manifest and beneficent Providence the uncomplaining endurance with which it was prosecuted to its consummation were only surpassed by the wisdom and patriotic spirit of concession which characterized all the counsels of the early fathers.

...But let not the foundation of our hope rest upon man's wisdom. It will not be sufficient that sectional prejudices find no place in the public deliberations. It will not be sufficient that the rash counsels of human passion are rejected. It must be felt that there is no national security but in the nation's humble, acknowledged dependence upon God and His overruling providence.

We have been carried in safety through a perilous crisis. Wise counsels, like those which gave us the Constitution, prevailed to uphold it. Let the period be remembered as an admonition, and not as an encouragement, in any section of the Union, to make experiments where experiments are fraught with such fearful hazard. Let it be impressed upon all hearts that, beautiful as our fabric is, no earthly power or wisdom could ever reunite its broken fragments. Standing, as I do, almost within view of the green slopes of Monticello, and, as it were, within reach of the tomb of Washington, with all the cherished memories of the past gathering around me like so many eloquent voices of exhortation from heaven, I can express no better hope for my country than that the kind Providence which smiled upon our fathers may enable their children to preserve the blessings they have inherited.

James Buchanan – 15th President (1857-1861)
Political Party: Democrat
Denomination: Presbyterian

Inaugural Address – 1857

In entering upon this great office I must humbly invoke the God of our fathers for wisdom and firmness to execute its high and responsible duties in such a manner as to restore harmony and ancient friendship among the people of the several States and to preserve our free institutions throughout many generations.

But such considerations, important as they are in

themselves, sink into insignificance when we reflect on the terrific evils which would result from disunion to every portion of the Confederacy--to the North, not more than to the South, to the East not more than to the West. These I shall not attempt to portray, because I feel an humble confidence that the kind Providence which inspired our fathers with wisdom to frame the most perfect form of government and union ever devised by man will not suffer it to perish until it shall have been peacefully instrumental by its example in the extension of civil and religious liberty throughout the world.

We ought to cultivate peace, commerce, and friendship with all nations, and this not merely as the best means of promoting our own material interests, but in a spirit of Christian benevolence toward our fellow-men, wherever their lot may be cast.

I shall now proceed to take the oath prescribed by the Constitution, whilst humbly invoking the blessing of Divine Providence on this great people.

Abraham Lincoln – 16th President (1861-1865)
Political Party: Republican
Denomination: Baptist/ Non-Denominational

Second Inaugural Address – 1865

Both read the same Bible and pray to the same God, and each invokes His aid against the other. It may seem strange that any men should dare to ask a just God's assistance in wringing their bread from the sweat of other men's faces, but let us judge not, that we be not judged. The prayers of both could not be answered. That of neither has been answered fully. The Almighty has His own purposes. "Woe unto the world because of offenses; for it must needs be that offenses come, but woe to that man by whom the offense cometh." If we shall suppose that American slavery is one of those offenses which, in the providence of God, must needs come, but which, having continued through His appointed time, He now wills to remove, and that He gives to both North and South this terrible war as the woe due to those by whom the offense came, shall we discern therein any departure from those divine attributes which the believers in a living God always ascribe to Him? Fondly do we hope, fervently do we pray, that this mighty scourge of war may speedily pass away. Yet, if God wills that it continue until all the wealth piled by the bondsman's two hundred and fifty years of unrequited toil shall be sunk, and until every drop of blood drawn with the lash shall be paid by another drawn with the sword, as was said three thousand years ago, so still it must be said "the judgments of the Lord are true and righteous altogether."

With malice toward none, with charity for all, with firmness in the right as God gives us to see the right, let us strive on to finish the work we are in, to bind up the nation's wounds, to care for him who shall have borne the battle and for his widow and his orphan, to do all which may achieve and cherish a just and lasting peace among ourselves and with all nations.

Andrew Johnson – 17th President (1865-1869)
Political Party: Union
Denomination: Non Denominational

Inaugural Address – 1865

To express gratitude to God in the name of the people for the preservation of the United States is my first duty in addressing you.

The Union of the United States of America was intended by its authors to last as long as the States themselves shall last. "The Union shall be perpetual" are the words of the Confederation. "To form a more perfect Union," by an ordinance of the people of the United States, is the declared purpose of the Constitution. The hand of Divine Providence was never more plainly visible in the affairs of men than in the framing and the adopting of that instrument.

Who of them will not now acknowledge, in the words of Washington, that "every step by which the people of the United States have advanced to the character of an independent nation seems to have been distinguished by some token of providential agency"? Who will not join with me in the prayer that the Invisible Hand which has led us through the clouds that gloomed around our path will so guide us onward to a perfect restoration of fraternal affection that we of this day may be able to transmit our great inheritance of State governments in all their rights, of the General Government in its whole constitutional vigor, to our posterity, and they to theirs through countless generations?

Ulysses S Grant - 18th President (1869-1877)
Political Party: Republican
Denomination: Presbyterian/ Methodist

Second Inaugural Address – 1873

Under Providence I have been called a second time to act as Executive over this great nation.

In future, while I hold my present office, the subject of acquisition of territory must have the support of the people before I will recommend any proposition looking to such acquisition. I say here, however, that I do not share in the apprehension held by many as to the danger of governments becoming weakened and destroyed by reason of their extension of territory. Commerce, education, and rapid transit of thought and matter by telegraph and steam have changed all this. Rather do I believe that our

Great Maker is preparing the world, in His own good time, to become one nation, speaking one language, and when armies and navies will be no longer required.

Rutherford B Hayes – 19th President (1877-1881)
Political Party: Republican
Denomination: Methodist

Inaugural Address – 1877

Looking for the guidance of that Divine Hand by which the destinies of nations and individuals are shaped, I call upon you, Senators, Representatives, judges, fellow-citizens, here and everywhere, to unite with me in an earnest effort to secure to our country the blessings, not only of material prosperity, but of justice, peace, and union--a union depending not upon the constraint of force, but upon the loving devotion of a free people; "and that all things may be so ordered and settled upon the best and surest foundations that peace and happiness, truth and justice, religion and piety, may be established among us for all generations."

James Garfield – 20th President (1881-1881)
Political Party: Republican
Denomination: Disciples of Christ

Inaugural Address – 1881

The emancipated race has already made remarkable progress. With unquestioning devotion to the Union, with a patience and gentleness not born of fear, they have "followed the light as God gave them to see the light."

It is the high privilege and sacred duty of those now living to educate their successors and fit them, by intelligence and virtue, for the inheritance which awaits them.

In this beneficent work sections and races should be forgotten and partisanship should be unknown. Let our people find a new meaning in the divine oracle which declares that "a little child shall lead them," for our own little children will soon control the destinies of the Republic.

My countrymen, we do not now differ in our judgment concerning the controversies of past generations, and fifty years hence our children will not be divided in their opinions concerning our controversies. They will surely bless their fathers and their fathers' God that the Union was preserved, that slavery was overthrown, and that both races were made equal before the law.

I shall greatly rely upon the wisdom and patriotism of Congress and of those who may share with me the responsibilities and duties of administration, and, above all, upon our efforts to promote the welfare of this great people and their Government I reverently invoke the support and blessings of Almighty God.

Chester A Arthur – 21st President (1881-1885)
Political Party: Republican
Denomination: Episcopalian

1st Annual Message – 1881

An appalling calamity has befallen the American people since their chosen representatives last met in the halls where you are now assembled. We might else recall with unalloyed content the rare prosperity with which throughout the year the nation has been blessed. Its harvests have been plenteous; its varied industries have thriven; the health of its people has been preserved; it has maintained with foreign governments the undisturbed relations of amity and peace. For these manifestations of His favor we owe to Him who holds our destiny in His hands the tribute of our grateful devotion.

To that mysterious exercise of His will which has taken from us the loved and illustrious citizen who was but lately the head of the nation we bow in sorrow and submission.

Grover Cleveland – 22nd and 24th President
(1885-1889 & 1893-1897)
Political Party: Democrat
Denomination: Presbyterian

1st Term Inaugural Address – 1885

And let us not trust to human effort alone, but humbly acknowledging the power and goodness of Almighty God, who presides over the destiny of nations, and who has at all times been revealed in our country's history, let us invoke His aid and His blessings upon our labors.

2nd Term Inaugural Address – 1893

In obedience of the mandate of my countrymen I am about to dedicate myself to their service under the sanction of a solemn oath. Deeply moved by the expression of confidence and personal attachment which has called me to this service, I am sure my gratitude can make no better return than the pledge I now give before God and these witnesses of unreserved and complete devotion to the interests and welfare of those who have honored me.

It can not be doubted that our stupendous achievements as a people and our country's robust strength have given rise to heedlessness of those laws governing our national health which we can no more evade than human life can escape the laws of God and nature.

Above all, I know there is a Supreme Being who rules the affairs of men and whose goodness and mercy have always followed the American people, and I know He will not turn from us now if we humbly and reverently seek His powerful aid.

Benjamin Harrison – 23rd President (1889-1893)
Political Party: Republican
Denomination: Presbyterian

Inaugural Address – 1889

Entering thus solemnly into covenant with each other, we may reverently invoke and confidently expect the favor and help of Almighty God--that He will give to me wisdom, strength, and fidelity, and to our people a spirit of fraternity and a love of righteousness and peace.

No other people have a government more worthy of their respect and love or a land so magnificent in extent, so pleasant to look upon, and so full of generous suggestion to enterprise and labor. God has placed upon our head a diadem and has laid at our feet power and wealth beyond definition or calculation. But we must not forget that we take these gifts upon the condition that justice and mercy shall hold the reins of power and that the upward avenues of hope shall be free to all the people.

William McKinley – 25th President (1897-1901)
Political Party: Republican
Denomination: Methodist

<u>1st Inaugural Address – 1897</u>

In obedience to the will of the people, and in their presence, by the authority vested in me by this oath, I assume the arduous and responsible duties of President of the United States, relying upon the support of my countrymen and invoking the guidance of Almighty God. Our faith teaches that there is no safer reliance than upon the God of our fathers, who has so singularly favored the American people in every national trial, and who will not forsake us so long as we obey His commandments and walk humbly in His footsteps.

Illiteracy must be banished from the land if we shall attain that high destiny as the foremost of the enlightened nations of the world which, under Providence, we ought to achieve.

Let me again repeat the words of the oath administered by the Chief Justice which, in their respective spheres, so far as applicable, I would have all my countrymen observe: "I will faithfully execute the office of President of the United States, and will, to the best of my ability, preserve, protect, and defend the Constitution of the United States." This is the obligation I have reverently taken before the Lord Most High. To keep it will be my single purpose, my constant prayer; and I shall confidently rely upon the forbearance and assistance of all the people in the discharge of my solemn responsibilities.

Theodore Roosevelt – 26th President (1901-1909)
Political Party: Republican
Denomination: Dutch Reformed / Episcopalian

<u>Inaugural Address – 1905</u>

No people on earth have more cause to be thankful than ours, and this is said reverently, in no spirit of boastfulness in our own strength, but with gratitude to the Giver of Good who has blessed us with the conditions which have enabled us to achieve so large a measure of well-being and of happiness. To us as a people it has been granted to lay the foundations of our national life in a new continent…

William Taft – 27th President (1909-1913)
Political Party: Republican
Denomination: Unitarian

<u>Inaugural Address – 1909</u>

Anyone who has taken the oath I have just taken must feel a heavy weight of responsibility. If not, he has no conception of the powers and duties of the office upon which he is about to enter, or he is lacking in a proper sense of the obligation which the oath imposes…

Having thus reviewed the questions likely to recur during my administration, and having expressed in a summary way the position which I expect to take in recommendations to Congress and in my conduct as an Executive, I invoke the considerate sympathy and support of my fellow-citizens and the aid of the Almighty God in the discharge of my responsible duties.

Woodrow Wilson – 28th President (1913-1921)
Political Party: Democrat
Denomination: Presbyterian

<u>Inaugural Address – 1917</u>

...We are being forged into a new unity amidst the fires that now blaze throughout the world. In their ardent heat we shall, in God's Providence, let us hope, be purged of faction and division, purified of the errant humors of party and of private interest, and shall stand forth in the days to come with a new dignity of national pride and spirit. Let each man see to it that the dedication is in his own heart, the high purpose of the nation in his own mind, ruler of his own will and desire.

I stand here and have taken the high and solemn oath to which you have been audience because the people of the United States have chosen me for this august delegation of power and have by their gracious judgment named me their leader in affairs.

I know now what the task means. I realize to the full the responsibility which it involves. I pray God I may be given the wisdom and the prudence to do my duty in the true spirit of this great people....

Warren Harding – 29th President (1921-1923)
Political Party: Republican
Denomination: Baptist

<u>Inaugural Address –1921</u>

Standing in this presence, mindful of the solemnity of this occasion, feeling the emotions which no one may know until he senses the great weight of responsibility for himself, I must utter my belief in the divine inspiration of the founding fathers. Surely there must have been God's intent in the making of this new-world Republic...

Service is the supreme commitment of life. I would rejoice to acclaim the era of the Golden Rule and crown it with the autocracy of service. I pledge an administration wherein all the agencies of Government are called to serve, and ever promote an understanding of Government purely as an expression of the popular will.

One cannot stand in this presence and be unmindful of the tremendous responsibility. The world upheaval has added heavily to our tasks. But with the realization comes the surge of high resolve, and there is reassurance in belief in the God-given destiny of our Republic. If I felt that there is to be sole responsibility in the Executive for the America of tomorrow I should shrink from the burden. But here are a hundred millions, with common concern and shared responsibility, answerable to God and country. The Republic summons them to their duty, and I invite co-operation.

I accept my part with single-mindedness of purpose and humility of spirit, and implore the favor and guidance of God in His Heaven. With these I am unafraid, and confidently face the future.

I have taken the solemn oath of office on that passage of Holy Writ wherein it is asked: "What doth the Lord require of thee but to do justly, and to love mercy, and to walk humbly with thy God?" This I plight to God and country.

Calvin Coolidge – 30th President (1923-1929)
Political Party: Republican
Denomination: Congregationalist

Inaugural Address – 1925

Peace will come when there is realization that only under a reign of law, based on righteousness and supported by the religious conviction of the brotherhood of man, can there be any hope of a complete and satisfying life. Parchment will fail, the sword will fail, it is only the spiritual nature of man that can be triumphant.

Here stands our country, an example of tranquillity at

home, a patron of tranquillity abroad. Here stands its Government, aware of its might but obedient to its conscience. Here it will continue to stand, seeking peace and prosperity, solicitous for the welfare of the wage earner, promoting enterprise, developing waterways and natural resources, attentive to the intuitive counsel of womanhood, encouraging education, desiring the advancement of religion, supporting the cause of justice and honor among the nations. America seeks no earthly empire built on blood and force. No ambition, no temptation, lures her to thought of foreign dominions. The legions which she sends forth are armed, not with the sword, but with the cross. The higher state to which she seeks the allegiance of all mankind is not of human, but of divine origin. She cherishes no purpose save to merit the favor of Almighty God.

Herbert Hoover – 31st President (1929-1933)
Political Party: Republican
Denomination: Quaker

Inaugural Address – 1929

This occasion is not alone the administration of the most sacred oath which can be assumed by an American citizen. It is a dedication and consecration under God to the highest office in service of our people. I assume this trust in the humility of knowledge that only through the guidance of Almighty Providence can I hope to discharge its ever-increasing burdens.

In the presence of my countrymen, mindful of the solemnity of this occasion, knowing what the task means and the responsibility which it involves, I beg your tolerance, your aid, and your cooperation. I ask the help of Almighty God in this service to my country to which you have called me.

Franklin D Roosevelt – 32nd President (1933-1945)
Political Party: Democrat
Denomination: Episcopalian

<u>4th Inaugural Address – 1945</u>

The Almighty God has blessed our land in many ways. He has given our people stout hearts and strong arms with which to strike mighty blows for freedom and truth. He has given to our country a faith which has become the hope of all peoples in an anguished world.

So we pray to Him now for the vision to see our way clearly--to see the way that leads to a better life for ourselves and for all our fellow men--to the achievement of His will to peace on earth.

<u>D-Day Prayer – 1945</u>

Last night, when I spoke with you about the fall of Rome, I knew at that moment that troops of the United States and our Allies were crossing the Channel in another and greater operation. It has come to pass with success thus far.

And so, in this poignant hour, I ask you to join with me in prayer:

Almighty God: our sons, pride of our Nation, this day have set upon a mighty endeavor, a struggle to preserve our Republic, our religion, and our civilization, and to set free a suffering humanity.

Lead them straight and true; give strength to their arms, stoutness to their hearts, steadfastness in their faith.

They will need Thy blessings. Their road will be long and hard. For the enemy is strong. He may hurl back our forces. Success may not come with rushing speed, but we shall return again and again; and we know that by Thy grace, and by the righteousness of our cause, our sons will triumph.

They will be sore tried, by night and by day, without rest--until the victory is won. The darkness will be rent by noise and flame. Men's souls will be shaken with the violences of war.

For these men are lately drawn from the ways of peace.

They fight not for the lust of conquest. They fight to end conquest. They fight to liberate. They fight to let justice arise, and tolerance and good will among all Thy people. They yearn but for the end of battle, for their return to the haven of home.

Some will never return. Embrace these, Father, and receive them, thy heroic servants, into Thy kingdom.

And for us at home--fathers, mothers, children, wives, sisters and brothers of brave men overseas--whose thoughts and prayers are ever with them--help us, Almighty God, to rededicate ourselves in renewed faith in Thee in this hour of great sacrifice.

Many people have urged that I call the Nation into a single day of special prayer. But because the road is long and the desire is great, I ask that our people devote themselves in a continuance of prayer. As we rise to each new day, and again when each day is spent, let words of prayer be on our lips, invoking Thy help to our efforts.

Give us strength, too--strength in our daily tasks, to redouble the contributions we make in the physical and the material support of our armed forces.

And let our hearts be stout, to wait out the long travail, to bear sorrows that may come, to impart our courage unto our sons wheresoever they may be.

And, O Lord, give us faith. Give us faith in Thee; faith in our sons; faith in each other; faith in our united crusade. Let not the keenness of our spirit ever be dulled. Let not the impacts of temporary events, of temporal matters of but fleeting moment--let not these deter us in our unconquerable purpose.

With Thy blessing, we shall prevail over the unholy forces of our enemy. Help us to conquer the apostles of greed and racial arrogancies. Lead us to the saving of our country, and with our sister nations into a world unity that will spell a sure peace--a peace invulnerable to the schemings of unworthy men. And a peace that will let all men live in freedom, reaping the just rewards of their honest toil. Thy will be done, Almighty God.

Harry S Truman – 33rd President (1945-1953)
Political Party: Democrat
Denomination: Baptist

Inaugural Address – 1949

The American people stand firm in the faith which has inspired this Nation from the beginning. We believe that all men have a right to equal justice under law and equal opportunity to share in the common good. We believe that all men have the right to freedom of thought and expression. We believe that all men are created equal because they are created in the image of God.

Steadfast in our faith in the Almighty, we will advance toward a world where man's freedom is secure.

To that end we will devote our strength, our resources, and our firmness of resolve. With God's help, the future of mankind will be assured in a world of justice, harmony, and peace.

Dwight Eisenhower – 34th President (1953-1961)
Political Party: Republican
Denomination: Presbyterian

1st Inaugural Address – 1953

My friends, before I begin the expression of those thoughts that I deem appropriate to this moment, would you permit me the privilege of uttering a little private prayer of my own. And I ask that you bow your heads:

Almighty God, as we stand here at this moment my future associates in the executive branch of government join me in beseeching that Thou will make full and complete our dedication to the service of the people in this throng, and their fellow citizens everywhere.

Give us, we pray, the power to discern clearly right from wrong, and allow all our words and actions to be governed thereby, and by the laws of this land. Especially we pray that our concern shall be for all the people regardless of station, race, or calling.

May cooperation be permitted and be the mutual aim of those who, under the concepts of our Constitution, hold to differing political faiths; so that all may work for the good of our beloved country and Thy glory. Amen.

In the swift rush of great events, we find ourselves groping to know the full sense and meaning of these times in which we live. In our quest of understanding, we beseech God's guidance...

At such a time in history, we who are free must proclaim anew our faith. This faith is the abiding creed of our fathers. It is our faith in the deathless dignity of man, governed by eternal moral and natural laws.

This faith defines our full view of life. It establishes, beyond debate, those gifts of the Creator that are man's inalienable rights, and that make all men equal in His sight.

It is because we, all of us, hold to these principles that the political changes accomplished this day do not imply turbulence, upheaval or disorder. Rather this change expresses a purpose of strengthening our dedication and devotion to the precepts of our founding documents, a conscious renewal of faith in our country and in the watchfulness of a Divine Providence.

And so each citizen plays an indispensable role. The productivity of our heads, our hands, and our hearts is the source of all the strength we can command, for both the enrichment of our lives and the winning of the peace.

No person, no home, no community can be beyond the reach of this call. We are summoned to act in wisdom and in conscience, to work with industry, to teach with persuasion, to preach with conviction, to weigh our every deed with care and with compassion. For this truth must be clear before us: whatever

America hopes to bring to pass in the world must first come to pass in the heart of America.

The peace we seek, then, is nothing less than the practice and fulfillment of our whole faith among ourselves and in our dealings with others. This signifies more than the stilling of guns, easing the sorrow of war. More than escape from death, it is a way of life. More than a haven for the weary, it is a hope for the brave.

This is the hope that beckons us onward in this century of trial. This is the work that awaits us all, to be done with bravery, with charity, and with prayer to Almighty God.

John F Kennedy - 35th President (1961-1963)
Political Party: Democrat
Denomination: Catholic

Inaugural Address – 1961

Vice President Johnson, Mr. Speaker, Mr. Chief Justice, President Eisenhower, Vice President Nixon, President Truman, reverend clergy, fellow citizens, we observe today not a victory of party, but a celebration of freedom--symbolizing an end, as well as a beginning--signifying renewal, as well as change. For I have sworn before you and Almighty God the same solemn oath our forebears prescribed nearly a century and three quarters ago.

The world is very different now. For man holds in his mortal hands the power to abolish all forms of human poverty and all forms of human life. And yet the same revolutionary beliefs for which our forebears fought are still at issue around the globe--the belief that the rights of man come not from the generosity of the state, but from the hand of God.

Let both sides unite to heed in all corners of the earth the command of Isaiah--to "undo the heavy burdens ... and to let the oppressed go free."

...Finally, whether you are citizens of America or citizens of the world, ask of us the same high standards of strength and sacrifice which we ask of you. With a good conscience our only sure reward, with history the final judge of our deeds, let us go forth to lead the land we love, asking His blessing and His help, but knowing that here on earth God's work must truly be our own.

Lyndon B. Johnson – 36th President (1963-1969)
Political Party: Democrat
Denomination: Disciples of Christ

Inaugural Address – 1965

My fellow countrymen, on this occasion, the oath I have taken before you and before God is not mine alone, but ours together. We are one nation and one people. Our fate as a nation and our future as a people rest not upon one citizen, but upon all citizens.

Under this covenant of justice, liberty, and union we have become a nation--prosperous, great, and mighty. And we have kept our freedom. But we have no promise from God that our greatness will endure. We have been allowed by Him to seek greatness with the sweat of our hands and the strength of our spirit.

For myself, I ask only, in the words of an ancient leader: "Give me now wisdom and knowledge, that I may go out and come in before this people: for who can judge this thy people, that is so great?"

Richard M Nixon – 37th President (1969-1974)
Political Party: Republican
Denomination: Quaker

<u>Inaugural address – 1969</u>

I have taken an oath today in the presence of God and my countrymen to uphold and defend the Constitution of the United States. To that oath I now add this sacred commitment: I shall consecrate my office, my energies, and all the wisdom I can summon, to the cause of peace among nations.

Let this message be heard by strong and weak alike:

The peace we seek to win is not victory over any other people, but the peace that comes "with healing in its wings"; with compassion for those who have suffered; with understanding for those who have opposed us; with the opportunity for all the peoples of this earth to choose their own destiny.

Only a few short weeks ago, we shared the glory of man's first sight of the world as God sees it, as a single sphere reflecting light in the darkness.

As the Apollo astronauts flew over the moon's gray surface on Christmas Eve, they spoke to us of the beauty of earth--and in that voice so clear across the lunar distance, we heard them invoke God's blessing on its goodness.

In that moment, their view from the moon moved poet Archibald MacLeish to write:

"To see the earth as it truly is, small and blue and beautiful in that eternal silence where it floats, is to see ourselves as riders on the earth together, brothers on that bright loveliness in the eternal cold--brothers who know now they are truly brothers."

In that moment of surpassing technological triumph, men turned their thoughts toward home and humanity--seeing in that far perspective that man's destiny on earth is not divisible; telling us that however far we reach into the cosmos, our destiny lies not in the stars but on Earth itself, in our own hands, in our own hearts.

We have endured a long night of the American spirit. But as our eyes catch the dimness of the first rays of dawn, let us not curse the remaining dark. Let us gather the light.

A Nation Under God

Our destiny offers, not the cup of despair, but the chalice of opportunity. So let us seize it, not in fear, but in gladness--and, "riders on the earth together," let us go forward, firm in our faith, steadfast in our purpose, cautious of the dangers; but sustained by our confidence in the will of God and the promise of man.

Gerald Ford – 38th President (1974-1977)
Political Party: Republican
Denomination: Episcopalian

Comments Upon Taking Office – 1974

I am acutely aware that you have not elected me as your President by your ballots, and so I ask you to confirm me as your President with your prayers. And I hope that such prayers will also be the first of many.

In the beginning, I asked you to pray for me. Before closing, I ask again your prayers, for Richard Nixon and for his family. May our former President, who brought peace to millions, find it for himself. May God bless and comfort his wonderful wife and daughters, whose love and loyalty will forever be a shining legacy to all who bear the lonely burdens of the White House.

I can only guess at those burdens, although I have witnessed at close hand the tragedies that befell three Presidents and the lesser trials of others.

With all the strength and all the good sense I have gained from life, with all the confidence my family, my friends, and my dedicated staff impart to me, and with the good will of countless Americans I have encountered in recent visits to 40 States, I now solemnly reaffirm my promise I made to you last December 6: to uphold the Constitution, to do what is right as God gives me to see the right, and to do the very best I can for America.

God helping me, I will not let you down.

James E Carter – 39th President (1977-1981)
Political Party: Democrat
Denomination: Baptist

Inaugural Address – 1977

Here before me is the Bible used in the inauguration of our first President, in 1789, and I have just taken the oath of office on the Bible my mother gave me a few years ago, opened to a timeless admonition from the ancient prophet Micah:
"He hath showed thee, O man, what is good; and what doth the Lord require of thee, but to do justly, and to love mercy, and to walk humbly with thy God." (Micah 6:8)

Let us learn together and laugh together and work together and pray together, confident that in the end we will triumph together in the right.

_____

Ronald Reagan – 40th President (1981-1989)
Political Party: Republican
Denomination: Presbyterian

2nd Inaugural Address – 1985

There is, however, one who is not with us today: Representative Gillis Long of Louisiana left us last night. I wonder if we could all join in a moment of silent prayer. (Moment of silent prayer.) Amen.

History is a ribbon, always unfurling; history is a journey. And as we continue our journey, we think of those who traveled before us. We stand together again at the steps of this symbol of our democracy--or we would have been standing at the steps if it hadn't gotten so cold. Now we are standing inside this symbol of our democracy. Now we hear again the echoes of our past: a general falls to his knees in the hard snow of Valley Forge; a lonely President paces the darkened halls, and ponders his struggle to preserve the Union; the men of the Alamo call out encouragement to each other; a settler pushes west and sings a song, and the song echoes out forever and fills the unknowing air.

It is the American sound. It is hopeful, big-hearted, idealistic, daring, decent, and fair. That's our heritage; that is our song. We sing it still. For all our problems, our differences, we are together as of old, as we raise our voices to the God who is the Author of this most tender music. And may He continue to hold us close as we fill the world with our sound--sound in unity, affection, and love--one people under God, dedicated to the dream of freedom that He has placed in the human heart, called upon now to pass that dream on to a waiting and hopeful world.

God bless you and may God bless America.

George Bush – 41st President (1989-1993)
Political Party: Republican
Denomination: Episcopalian

Inaugural Address – 1989

I have just repeated word for word the oath taken by George Washington 200 years ago, and the Bible on which I placed my hand is the Bible on which he placed his.

And my first act as President is a prayer. I ask you to bow your heads:

Heavenly Father, we bow our heads and thank You for Your love. Accept our thanks for the peace that yields this day and the shared faith that makes its continuance likely. Make us strong to do Your work, willing to heed and hear Your will, and write on our hearts these words: "Use power to help people." For we are given power not to advance our own purposes, nor to make a great show in the world, nor a name. There is but one just use of power, and it is to serve people. Help us to remember it, Lord. Amen.

And so, there is much to do; and tomorrow the work begins. I do not mistrust the future; I do not fear what is ahead. For our problems are large, but our heart is larger. Our challenges are great, but our will is greater. And if our flaws are endless, God's love is truly boundless.

Thank you. God bless you and God bless the United States of America.

William J Clinton – 42nd President (1993-2001)
Political Party: Democrat
Denomination: Baptist

Inaugural Address – 1992

And so, my fellow Americans, at the edge of the 21st Century, let us begin with energy and hope, with faith and discipline, and let us work until the work is done. The scripture says, "And let us not be weary in well-doing , for in due season, we shall reap, if we faint not."
From this joyful mountaintop of celebration, we hear a call to service in the valley. We have heard the trumpets. We have changed the guard. And now, each in our own way, and with God's help, we must answer the call.
Thank you and God bless you all.

George W. Bush – 43rd President (2001-2008)
Political Party: Republican
Denomination: Methodist

Inaugural Address – 2001

America, at its best, is compassionate. In the quiet of American conscience, we know that deep, persistent poverty is unworthy of our nation's promise. And whatever our views of its cause, we can agree that children at risk are not at fault. Abandonment and abuse are not acts of God, they are failures of love.

Government has great responsibilities for public safety and public health, for civil rights and common schools. Yet compassion is the work of a nation, not just a government. And some needs and hurts are so deep they will only respond to a mentor's touch or a pastor's prayer. Church and charity, synagogue and mosque lend our communities their humanity, and they will have an honored place in our plans and in our laws. Many in our country do not know the pain of poverty, but we can listen to those who do. And I can pledge our nation to a goal: When we see that wounded traveler on the road to Jericho, we will not pass to the other side.

Americans are generous and strong and decent, not because we believe in ourselves, but because we hold beliefs beyond ourselves. When this spirit of citizenship is missing, no government program can replace it. When this spirit is present, no wrong can stand against it. After the Declaration of Independence was signed, Virginia statesman John Page wrote to Thomas Jefferson: "We know the race is not to the swift nor the battle to the strong. Do you not think an angel rides in the whirlwind and directs this storm?"
Much time has passed since Jefferson arrived for his inauguration. The years and changes accumulate. But the themes of this day he would know: our nation's grand story of courage and its simple dream of dignity.

We are not this story's author, who fills time and eternity with his purpose. Yet his purpose is achieved in our duty, and our duty is fulfilled in service to one another.

Never tiring, never yielding, never finishing, we renew that purpose today, to make our country more just and generous, to affirm the dignity of our lives and every life.

This work continues. This story goes on. And an angel still rides in the whirlwind and directs this storm.

God bless you all, and God bless America.

Barack Obama – 44rd President (2009-)
Political Party: Democrat
Denomination: Non-Denominational Christian

The time has come to reaffirm our enduring spirit; to choose our better history; to carry forward that precious gift, that noble idea passed on from generation to generation: the God-given promise that all are equal, all are free, and all deserve a chance to pursue their full measure of happiness.

… This is the source of our confidence -- the knowledge that God calls on us to shape an uncertain destiny. This is the meaning of our liberty and our creed, why men and women and children of every race and every faith can join in celebration across this magnificent mall; and why a man whose father less than 60 years ago might not have been served in a local restaurant can now stand before you to take a most sacred oath.

… Let it be said by our children's children that when we were tested we refused to let this journey end, that we did not turn back nor did we falter; and with eyes fixed on the horizon and God's grace upon us, we carried forth that great gift of freedom and delivered it safely to future generations.

Thank you. God bless you. And God bless the United States of America.

An American Religious Heritage

In order to make a case that there is no religious heritage in the United States of America, one would have to avoid the overwhelming textual history stating the opposite. Throughout our history, politicians and citizens have relied on the love of the Lord to care for their families and national goals.

In the next pages, you'll see selections from our national religious heritage. These compliment the Presidential and State quotes, in prior pages, that show the same passions of the people for God.

You will see that a religious foundation and belief in providence backed our nation's founding. The founders were quick to acknowledge where they got their success – in God.

God was also present in the westward expansion of the nation and the national crisis over the civil war, on both sides.

Later, when World War I tried our nation, there were also multiple expressions of faith during that trying time. Consistent with our national history, the soldiers and their families, when faced with danger, relied upon the Lord to see them through.

Finally, I have included an official proclamation by Ronald Reagan recognizing the bible in the history and heritage of the USA.

These examples given in this chapter are a very small portion of similar texts and quotes establishing the same principle. The testimony of a nation "under God" is full of providential success.

Continental Congress Thanksgiving Proclamaton – 1776

In CONGRESS,
SATURDAY, March 16, 1776.

IN times of impending calamity and distress; when the Liberties of America are imminently endangered by the secret machinations and open assaults of an insidious and vindictive Administration, it becomes the indispensible duty of these hitherto free and happy Colonies, with true penitence of heart, and the most reverent devotion, publickly to acknowledge the over ruling providence of God; to confess and deplore our offences against him; and to supplicate his interposition for averting the threatened danger, and prospering our strenuous efforts in the cause of Freedom, Virtue and Posterity.

The Congress therefore, considering the warlike preparations of the British Ministry to subvert our invaluable rights and privileges, and to reduce us by fire and sword, by the savages of the wilderness and our own domestics, to the most abject and ignominious bandage: Desirous, at the same time, to have people of all ranks and degrees, duly impressed with a solemn of God's superintending providence, and of their duty devoutly to rely in all their lawful enterprizes of his aid and direction--do earnestly recommend, that FRIDAY, the seventeenth day of May next, be observed by the said Colonies as a day of HUMILIATION, FASTING, and PRAYER; that we may with united hearts confess and bewail our manifold sins and transgressions, and by a sincere, repentance and amendment of life, appease his righteous displeasure and through the merits and mediation of Jesus Christ, obtain his pardon and forgiveness; humbly imploring his assistance to frustrate the cruel purposes of our unnatural enemies; and by inclining their hearts to justice and benevolence, prevent the further effusion of kindred blood. But if continuing deaf to the voice of reason and humanity, and inflexibly bent on desolation and war, they constrain us to repel their hostile invasions by open resistance, it may please the Lord of Hosts, the God of Armies, to animate our Officers and Soldiers with invincible to guard and protect them in the day of battle, and to crown the Continental arms by sea and land with victory and success: Earnestly beseeching him to bless

our civil Rulers and the Representatives of the People in their
several Assemblies and Conventions; to preserve and strengthen
their Union, to inspire them with an ardent disinterested love of
their Country; to give wisdom and stability to their Councils; and
direct them to the most efficacious measures for establishing the
Rights of America on the most honorable and permanent basis--
that he would be graciously pleased to bless all his People in these
Colonies with Health and Plenty, and grant that a spirit of
incorruptible Patriotism and of pure undefiled Religion may
unversally prevail; and this Continent be speedily restored to the
blessings of Peace and Liberty, and enabled to transmit them
inviolate to the latest Posterity. And it is recommended to
Christians of all denominations to assemble for Public Worship, and
abstain from servile Labour on the said Day.

Declaration of Independence – July 4, 1776

When in the Course of human events, it becomes necessary
for one people to dissolve the political bands which have
connected them with another, and to assume among the powers
of the earth, the separate and equal station to which the Laws of
Nature and of Nature's God entitles them...

We hold these truths to be self-evident, that all men are
created equal, that they are endowed by their Creator with
certain inalienable Rights...

And for the support of this Declaration, with a firm reliance on
the protection of divine Providence, we mutually pledge to each
other our Lives, our Fortunes, and our sacred Honor.

Samuel Adams letter to John Sullivan – 1776

It is my most fervent prayer to Almighty God, that he would direct and prosper the Councils of America, inspire her Armies with true Courage, shield them in every Instance of Danger and lead them on to Victory & Tryumph. I am yr affectionate Friend, S.A.

King of France to Congress – 1778

The interest that we take in the prosperity of your Republic is our warrant for the pleasure which we have in repeating to you the assurances of our esteem and of our constant affection. Moreover, we pray God that he may keep you, very dear and great friends and allies, under his holy and worthy protection.
Louis.

Continental Congress Thanksgiving Proclamation – 1779

The committee appointed to prepare a recommendation to the several states to set apart a day of fasting humiliation and prayer, brought in a draught, which was taken into consideration, and agreed to as follows:
Whereas, in just punishment of our manifold transgressions, it hath pleased the Supreme Disposer of all events to visit these United States with a destructive calamitous war, through which His divine Providence hath, hitherto, in a wonderful manner, conducted us, so that we might acknowledge that the race is not to the swift, nor the battle to the strong: and whereas, there is but too much Reason to fear that notwithstanding the chastisements received and benefits bestowed, too few have been sufficiently awakened to a sense of their guilt, or warmed our Bosoms with gratitude, or taught to amend their lives and turn from their sins, that so He might turn from His wrath. And whereas, from a consciousness of what we have merited at His hands, and an

93

apprehension that the malevolence of our disappointed enemies, like the incredulity of Pharaoh, may be used as the scourge of Omnipotence to vindicate his slighted Majesty, there is reason to fear that he may permit much of our land to become the prey of the spoiler, and the Blood of the innocent be poured out that our borders to be ravaged, and our habitations destroyed:

Resolved, That it be recommended to the several states to appoint the first Thursday in May next, to be a day of fasting, Thanksgiving humiliation and prayer to Almighty God, that he will be pleased to avert those impending calamities which we have but too well deserved: that he will grant us his grace to repent of our sins, and amend our lives, according to his holy word: that he will continue that wonderful protection which hath led us through the paths of danger and distress: that he will be a husband to the widow and a father to the fatherless children, who weep over the barbarities of a savage enemy: that he will grant us patience in suffering, and fortitude in adversity: that he will inspire us with humility and moderation, and gratitude in prosperous circumstances: that he will give wisdom to our councils, firmness to our resolutions, and victory to our arms That he will have Mercy on our Foes, and graciously forgive them, and turn their Hearts from Enmity to Love.

That he will bless the labours of the husbandman, and pour forth abundance, so that we may enjoy the fruits of the earth in due season.

That he will cause union, harmony, and mutual confidence to prevail throughout these states: that he will bestow on our great ally all those blessings which may enable him to be gloriously instrumental in protecting the rights of mankind, and promoting the happiness of his subjects and advancing the Peace and Liberty of Nations. That he will give to both Parties to this Alliance, Grace to perform with Honor and Fidelity their National Engagements. That he will bountifully continue his paternal care to the commander in chief, and the officers and soldiers of the United States: that he will grant the blessings of peace to all contending nations, freedom to those who are in bondage, and comfort to the afflicted: that he will diffuse useful knowledge, extend the influence of true religion, and give us that peace of mind, which the world cannot give: that he will be our shield in the

94

day of battle, our comforter in the hour of death, and our kind parent and merciful judge through time and through eternity.

Henry Laurens letter to John Laurens – 1779

Go on my Son, Love & be ready at all times to bleed for your Country. "If we do meet again, why, we shall smile, if not, why, then our fasting was well made." I pray that Holy God in whom we confide, of whose attributes nor Brutus nor Cassius had just conceptions, to continue to you his mercies & his protection; in him alone I trust in my daily prayers for the salvation of my Country.
Henry Laurens

I've decided to include the entire letter from Elias Boudinot to his daughter, as I think it depicts the value of religion and the motivation of education held by some of our country's founders in the late 1700s.

Elias Boudinot letter to Susan Boudinot – 1782

My dearest Susan. Philadelphia Octr. 30th. 1782
Your Letter of the 19th Instt. lies unanswered, altho' I am still a Letter ahead of you, but as it is said, in an invaluable Book of Antiquity, that the Elder shall serve the Younger, perhaps you may think it right, that I should go on, bringing you in debt.

I propose this Letter as a serious one--I have for some time past been led by Circumstances, to reflect more seriously on the prospect of you launching into life, and leaving your Fathers Roof, as well as his immediate Protection & Guardianship.

I have reflected how far, I have done my Duty in executing the Trust committed to me, by the great Governor of the Universe in your Education--in a proper Provision for you in Life, in preparing you for usefulness in whatever Station it may please God to call you--and laying a rational foundation, by the aid of Divine Grace, for your enjoyment of a glorious & happy Immortality in the life to Come. Through the unmerited Blessing of a kind Providence, I cannot blame myself greatly, for any deficiency in your Education and Provision for Life--Nature wants but little and not that little long. I have confidence in you, that if you make good use of and continue improving those Abilities & that knowledge you now possess, your usefulness in this Life under God, may be of some Importance to your Fellow Creatures.

But my dear Child, all these are but secondary Objects. How stands it as to your preparation for and hope in the prospects of a joyfull Immortality--I can assure you in all the Sincerity of Truth, that you have been from your first Conception, dedicated to God, as his peculiar Property. At your Birth (which was a Miracle of Mercy, and deserves your whole Soul, as a living Monument thereof) you was repeatedly, by the most solemn Acts of religious Worship in the fear of God, given up to him. Your Baptism in the Face of the Church of Christ, was an Express Covenant with God in Christ on your Behalf, by which you Altogether became the Lord's--Your Parents became bound on your Part, and I devoutly trust that the Contract stands ratified in Heaven. You have been instructed from your Childhood in the knowledge of your Lost State by Nature--the absolute necessity of a Change of Heart, and an entire renovation of Soul, to the Image of Jesus Christ--of Salvation, thro' his meritorious Righteousness only--and the indispensable necessity of personal Holiness without which no man shall see the Lord. You are well acquainted that the most perfect & consummate Doctrinal Knowledge, is of no avail, without it operates on & sincerely affects the Heart--Changes the Practice--and totally influences the Will-- and that without the almighty Power of the Spirit of God, enlightening your Mind, subduing your Will, and continually drawing you to himself--you can do nothing. Altho' at the same Time, your own Constant unwearied Endeavours after Holiness and perpetual Applications to a merciful Saviour for this Aid, are as necessary as if you could accomplish your own Salvation by your own Works.

Blessed be God, this has been your happy Lot, but my dearest Susan, all our Tears, Prayers, Dedications, Instructions, Example, & Admonitions will not accomplish the Event so devoutly

96

to be wished. What have You done, in your own Person, since you
have come to the Age of discretion? Have you confirmed the all
gracious Covenant. Have you justified your Parents, in the
multiplied Acts of devoting you to God? They have travailed in
Birth a second time with you, till you should be born again to
newness of Life. Your baptismal Covenant was the Act of your
Parents, in your Name & Behalf, but it is high Time, that this Act of
your Parents should be acknowledged & renewed by you, in the
solemn dedication of yourself in the Lords Supper. This is an
Ordinance designed as a solemn Seal of the same Covenant, as if
designed by your Baptism. They are both Seals of the same
Covenant, and a worthy Subject, of one is a worthy subject of the
other. I have a most earnest desire, that this important Event in
your Life, should take place before you launch into the world, and
leave your Father's assiduous care, that he may be blessed, with
seeing the work completed, as far as human endeavours can go.
That you may go forth under the protection of the God of Heaven,
as his peculiar inheritance by your own Act, in Compliance with his
positive Command "Do this in remembrance of me." I was led to
this train of reflection by a Sermon I lately heard on this Subject--
the only one I remember that fully came up to my Sentiments and
which I verily believe is founded on the Truth of the Gospell. My
Anxiety for your accomplishing (and that without delay) your
whole Duty, made me wish most heartily, you could have heard it
delivered, because it might have removed all scruples, which too
often injure young & tender minds. To shew you my warmest
desires for your Spiritual Growth in Grace and that you may go
from under my immediate Care, the Subject of the divine special
Grace & Government, I have amidst all the Variety of my
important concerns, by taking from the Hours of the Night,
endeavoured to commit the Sermon to Writing for your careful
perusal & Improvement. Read it with Attention--Consider it well--It
is the Truth and the Truth will set you free. Be not deceived or
discouraged. You are in Covenant with God by the Act of your
Parents--I hope by your own private Acts. Be not afraid to go to
him as you[r] Father--your Friend & your God. Remember that it is in
the use of his own Appointed Means, that we are to expect the
Blessing. And may the God of your Parents (for many Generations
past) seal Instruction to your Soul and lead you to himself thro' the

Blood of his too greatly despised Son, who notwithstanding, is still reclaiming the World to God thro' that Blood, not imputing to them their Sins. To him be Glory forever.

I have wrote this in Congress, amidst a Warm debate, to which I have been obliged to attend, at the same time, therefore, you must make the necessary corrections yourself.

My kind Love to all who think it worth while to inquire after me. Am my Dearest Susan, Your very Afft. Father, Elias Boudinot

---

Constitutional Convention – 1787
Benjamin Franklin

In this situation of this Assembly, groping as it were in the dark to find political truth, and scarce able to distinguish it when presented to us, how has it happened, Sir, that we have not hitherto once thought of humbly applying to the Father of lights to illuminate our understandings?

In the beginning of the Contest with G. Britain, when we were sensible of danger we had daily prayer in this room for the divine protection.--Our prayers, Sir, were heard, and they were graciously answered. All of us who were engaged in the struggle must have observed frequent instances of a Superintending providence in our favor.

To that kind providence we owe this happy opportunity of consulting in peace on the means of establishing our future national felicity. And have we now forgotten that powerful friend? or do we imagine that we no longer need his assistance?

I have lived, Sir, a long time, and the longer I live, the more convincing proofs I see of this truth--that God governs in the affairs of men. And if a sparrow cannot fall to the ground without his notice, is it probable that an empire can rise without his aid?

We have been assured, Sir, in the sacred writings, that "except the Lord build the House they labour in vain that build it." I firmly believe this; and I also believe that without his concurring aid we shall succeed in this political building no better than the Builders of Babel: We shall be divided by our little partial local interests; our projects will be confounded, and we ourselves shall become

98

a reproach and bye word down to future ages. And what is worse, mankind may hereafter from this unfortunate instance, despair of establishing Governments by Human Wisdom and leave it to chance, war and conquest.

I therefore beg leave to move--that henceforth prayers imploring the assistance of Heaven, and its blessings on our deliberations, be held in this Assembly every morning before we proceed to business, and that one or more of the Clergy of this City be requested to officiate in that service.

Presidential Thanksgiving Proclamation – George Washington 1789

Whereas it is the duty of all Nations to acknowledge the providence of Almighty God, to obey his will, to be grateful for his benefits, and humbly to implore his protection and favor-- and whereas both Houses of Congress have by their joint Committee requested me to recommend to the People of the United States a day of public thanksgiving and prayer to be observed by acknowledging with grateful hearts the many signal favors of Almighty God especially by affording them an opportunity peaceably to establish a form of government for their safety and happiness.

Now therefore I do recommend and assign Thursday the 26th day of November next to be devoted by the People of these States to the service of that great and glorious Being, who is the beneficent Author of all the good that was, that is, or that will be-- That we may then all unite in rendering unto him our sincere and humble thanks--for his kind care and protection of the People of this Country previous to their becoming a Nation--for the signal and manifold mercies, and the favorable interpositions of his Providence which we experienced in the course and conclusion of the late war--for the great degree of tranquility, union, and plenty, which we have since enjoyed--for the peaceable and rational manner, in which we have been enabled to establish constitutions of government for our safety and happiness, and particularly the national One now lately instituted--for the civil and religious liberty with which we are blessed; and the means we have of acquiring and diffusing useful knowledge; and in general for all the great and various favors which he hath been pleased to confer upon us.

[A]nd also that we may then unite in most humbly offering our prayers and supplications to the great Lord and Ruler of Nations and beseech him to pardon our national and other transgressions-- to enable us all, whether in public or private stations, to perform our several and relative duties properly and punctually--to render our national government a blessing to all the people, by constantly being a Government of wise, just, and constitutional laws, discreetly and faithfully executed and obeyed--to protect and guide all Sovereigns and Nations (especially such as have shewn kindness unto us) and to bless them with good government, peace, and concord--To promote the knowledge and practice of true religion and virtue, and the encrease of science among them and us--and generally to grant unto all Mankind such a degree of temporal prosperity as he alone knows to be best.

Given under my hand at the City of New York the third day of October in the year of our Lord 1789.

Go: Washington

America (My Country 'Tis of Thee) – 1832
By: Samuel Francis Smith

Fourth Verse:

Our fathers' God, to thee,
Author of liberty,
To Thee we sing;
Long may our land be bright,
With freedom's holy light;
Protect us by thy might,
Great God, our King.

100

Confederate Congress Journal Prayers to God – 1861

The Chair presented to Congress a communication and resolutions from the Baptist convention of the State of Georgia; which were, on motion of Mr. Wright, ordered to be spread upon the Journal, and are as follows:

Athens, Ga., April 29, 1861.

Sir: I have the honor of transmitting to you the accompanying resolutions unanimously passed on Saturday last by the Baptist convention of the State of Georgia, with the request that you will present them to the Congress over which you preside.

That God will direct and bless the councils of the Congress and the Confederate Government is the prayer of the Baptist convention of Georgia, and of none more sincerely than your obedient servant,

N. M. CRAWFORD,

Chairman of the Committee.

Gettysburg Address – Abraham Lincoln – 1863

Fourscore and seven years ago our fathers brought forth on this continent a new nation, conceived in liberty, and dedicated to the proposition that all men are created equal.

It is rather for us to be here dedicated to the great task remaining before us - that from these honored dead we take increased devotion to that cause for which they gave the last full measure of devotion - that we here highly resolve that these dead shall not have died in vain - that this nation, under God, shall have a new birth of freedom and that government of the people, by the people, for the people, shall not perish from the earth.

Washington Territory's first Telegraph to Washington D.C. – 1864

Washington Territory this day sends her first telegraphic dispatch Greeting yourself Washington City & the Whole United States with our sincere prayer to Almighty God that his richest blessings spiritual & temporal may rest upon & perpetuate the whole of our beloved Country, that his omnipresent power may bless her & defend the President of the U S, our brave army & Navy, and Congress & every Department of the National Government forever.

Stars and Stripes World War I - 1918-1919

Stars and Stripes had many articles mentioning God and prayer over the course of World War I. Below are only a few samples of these expressions of faith.

A prayer of Victory

All Things come to Thee, O God!
Thine own, to Thee Remain.
Through deolate the way we trod,
We saw Thee in our pain.

The beauty and the might of truth,
The starlight way of right
Were fast before our age and youth,
Their vision and their light.

The deaths we died, the blood we bled,
Was in the faith we hold.
We mourn not those whose souls have fled
Into that gloried fold.

Their sanctus rings eternally,
Their is a deathless fame.
They died that this, Thine earth, might be

Still worthy of Thine name.
-Paul Hyde Bonner, 2 Lt., D.C.I.

~ ~   ~   ~   ~   ~   ~   ~

A Sister's Prayer

Dear God, if I were but a boy,
I would enlist at once and fight
For Liberty, Oh, what a joy
To give my life for Thee and Right!

My hand, O God, I shall not give
To one who has not taken part
In this great war that Freedom live!
A soldier, Lord, shall have my heart!

A Veteran's Prayer

Alas! my God, I'm sixty-one;
Though used to armies and the fray,
'Too old,' they say, 'to shoulder gun;'
'Tis hard to only watch and pray.

But I have sent my son to France,
My flesh and blood to fight for me.
O happy son! This is your chance
To die for God and Liberty!
-Thomas F. Coakley, Lt. Chaplain

~ ~   ~   ~   ~   ~   ~   ~

A chaplain's prayer

O Lord, I am not worthy to
Be found amid these reddened hands
Who offer an atoning due,
Themselves, to Thee, great martyr bands.

Let me but kiss the ground they tread,
And breathe a prayer above their sod,
And gather up the drops they shed,
These heroes in the cause of God.
-Thomas F. Coakley, Lt. Chaplain

~ ~   ~   ~   ~   ~   ~   ~

A soldier's Prayer

O God, protect my Mother dear,
Who toils and suffers more than I.
Her love of country sent me here;
That she may live, I will to die!

I'm ready, Lord; take Thou my soul
A hostage, let the pact be made;
'Twas she who urged me to the goal,
A partner in this last Crusade.
-Thomas F Coakley, Lt. Chaplain.

~ ~   ~   ~   ~   ~   ~   ~

A Battle Prayer

Alone upon a hill I stand
O'erlooking trench and No Man's Land;
In night's black skies, like Northern Lights,
Pale flashes rise to mark the heights
Where Death's dark angels bear away
The souls of men who die today.

Jesus of Nazareth, from Thy cross
Look down and comfort those who loss
And scream in pain and anguish dread
In No Man's Land among the dead;
Have pity for the wounds they bear,
Jesus of Nazareth, hear my prayer.

On Calvary, as the hours dragged,
From cruel nails Thy body sagged.
Yet in that agony, O Lord,
Thou didst give blessed comfort t'ward
One suffering soul who with Thee died;
He who for sin was crucified.

Out there lie men who die for right –
O Christ, be merciful tonight;
Wilt Thou who stilled the troubled seas
Stretch forth Thy hand their pain to ease,
Thy sons whose feet so bravely trod
Earth's battlefields, O Son of God?
-Brainerd Taylor, Major USA

Year of the bible proclamation – 1983

By the President of the United States of America
Of the many influences that have shaped the United States of America into a distinctive Nation and people, none may be said to be more fundamental and enduring than the Bible.

Deep religious beliefs stemming from the Old and New Testaments of the Bible inspired many of the early settlers of our country, providing them with the strength, character, convictions, and faith necessary to withstand great hardship and danger in this new and rugged land. These shared beliefs helped forge a sense of common purpose among the widely dispersed colonies -- a sense of community which laid the foundation for the spirit of nationhood that was to develop in later decades.

The Bible and its teachings helped form the basis for the Founding Fathers' abiding belief in the inalienable rights of the individual, rights which they found implicit in the Bible's teachings of the inherent worth and dignity of each individual. This same sense of man patterned the convictions of those who framed the English system of law inherited by our own Nation, as well as the ideals set forth in the Declaration of Independence and the

Constitution.

For centuries the Bible's emphasis on compassion and love for our neighbor has inspired institutional and governmental expressions of benevolent outreach such as private charity, the establishment of schools and hospitals, and the abolition of slavery.

Many of our greatest national leaders -- among them Presidents Washington, Jackson, Lincoln, and Wilson -- have recognized the influence of the Bible on our country's development. The plainspoken Andrew Jackson referred to the Bible as no less than ``the rock on which our Republic rests.'' Today our beloved America and, indeed, the world, is facing a decade of enormous challenge. As a people we may well be tested as we have seldom, if ever, been tested before. We will need resources of spirit even more than resources of technology, education, and armaments. There could be no more fitting moment than now to reflect with gratitude, humility, and urgency upon the wisdom revealed to us in the writing that Abraham Lincoln called ``the best gift God has ever given to man . . . But for it we could not know right from wrong.''

The Congress of the United States, in recognition of the unique contribution of the Bible in shaping the history and character of this Nation, and so many of its citizens, has by Senate Joint Resolution 165 authorized and requested the President to designate the year 1983 as the ``Year of the Bible.''

Now, Therefore, I, Ronald Reagan, President of the United States of America, in recognition of the contributions and influence of the Bible on our Republic and our people, do hereby proclaim 1983 the Year of the Bible in the United States. I encourage all citizens, each in his or her own way, to reexamine and rediscover its priceless and timeless message.

In Witness Whereof, I have hereunto set my hand this third day of February, in the year of our Lord nineteen hundred and eighty-three, and of the Independence of the United States of America the two hundred and seventh.

Ronald Reagan

Religion in Government Today

Every day, citizens throughout our land encounter public displays of religion officially established and sanctioned by our government. Even the most ardent separationists (desiring the separation of religion and state) will admit to an existing concept called "civic religion" as being legal in our land. This concept holds that certain religious terms and phrases have been said so often through our history that they have lost their religious value and have become non-religious expressions of patriotism and tradition.

When you handle money, you will see a religious expression on it. If you have ever been at the opening of Congress or the Supreme Court, you hear a religious expression. The swearing in of governmental officers has a religious expression. The Pledge of Allegiance contains a religious expression.

Probably the most obvious official religious expression is chaplains. Chaplains exist in every governmental branch. What the separationists don't tell you is that the issue of chaplains has already been brought to the Supreme Court, and they found them constitutional. In the following pages, you will read some quotes from that case.

A public expression of religion doesn't promote a specific religious view anymore than officially paid discussion of evolution promotes non-religion. We still have the freedom to believe whatever we want and are not punished for that chosen belief. However, official censorship of religious expression would send an official message of hostility to religion. May the freedom of religious expression, even by those in government, be protected.

A Nation Under God

Public Religious Expressions

The following are only a few places or positions that you can see official governmental recognition of God by the government.

<u>US Army Hymn</u>

March along, sing our song,
With the Army of the free
Count the brave, count the true,
Who have fought to victory
We're the Army and proud of our name
We're the Army and proudly proclaim

First to fight for the right,
And to build the Nation's might,
And The Army Goes Rolling Along
Proud of all we have done,
Fighting till the battle's done,
And the Army Goes Rolling Along.

Then it's Hi! Hi! Hey!
The Army's on its way.
Count off the cadence loud and strong,
For where e'er we go,
You will always know
That The Army Goes Rolling Along.

Valley Forge, Custer's ranks,
San Juan Hill and Patton's tanks,
And the Army went rolling along
Minute men, from the start,
Always fighting from the heart,
And the Army keeps rolling along.

Men in rags, men who froze,
Still that Army met its foes,
And the Army went rolling along.
Faith in God, then we're right,
And we'll fight with all our might,
As the Army keeps rolling along.

US Air Force Hymn

Lord, guard and guide the men who fly
Through the great spaces of the sky;
Be with them traversing the air
In darkening storms or sunshine fair. Amen.

Thou who dost keep with tender might
The balanced birds in all their flight,
Thou of the tempered winds, be near,
That, having Thee, they know no fear.

Control their minds with instinct fit
What time, adventuring, they quit
The firm security of land;
Grant steadfast eye and skillful hand.

Aloft in solitudes of space,
Uphold them with Thy saving grace.
O God, protect the men who fly
Thru lonely ways beneath the sky. Amen.

US Navy Hymn

Stand Navy down the field, sails set to the sky.
We'll never change our course, so Army you steer shy-y-y-y.
Roll up the score, Navy, Anchors Aweigh.
Sail Navy down the field and sink the Army, sink the Army Grey.

Get underway, Navy, Decks cleared for the fray,
We'll hoist true Navy Blue So Army down your Grey-y-y-y.
Full speed ahead, Navy; Army heave to,
Furl Black and Grey and Gold and hoist the Navy, hoist the Navy Blue

Blue of the Seven Seas; Gold of God's great sun
Let these our colors be Till all of time be done-n-n-ne,
By Severn shore we learn Navy's stern call:
Faith, courage, service true With honor over, honor over all.

US Marines Hymn

From the Halls of Montezuma,
To the Shores of Tripoli;
We fight our country's battles
In the air, on land, and sea;
First to fight for right and freedom
And to keep our honor clean;
We are proud to claim the title
Of UNITED STATES MARINES.

Our flag's unfurled to every breeze,
From dawn to setting sun;
We have fought in every clime and place

Where we could take a gun;
In the snow of far off northern lands
And in sunny tropic scenes;
You will find us always on the job --
The UNITED STATES MARINES.

Here's health to you and to our Corps
Which we are proud to serve;
In many a strife we've fought for life
And never lost our nerve;
If the Army and the Navy
Ever look on Heaven's scenes;
They will find the streets are guarded
By UNITED STATES MARINES.

US Coast Guard Hymn

Eternal Father, Lord of Hosts
Watch o'er the ones who guard our coasts
Protect them from the raging seas
And give them light and life and peace.
Grant them from thy great throne above
The shield and shelter of thy love.
Lord, guard and guide the ones who fly
Through the great spaces in the sky
Be with them always in the air,
In darken storms or sunlight fair,
Oh, hear us when we lift our prayer,
For those in peril in the air!
Grant to them Your eternal peace, Oh Lord,
For they have followed your commandment,
That No Greater Love has he, who would give up his life for another.
Amen

A Nation Under God

<u>National Motto / On our Coins</u>

This phrase was Established as our National Motto by P.L. 84-140, a joint resolution of the 84th congress, which was signed by President Eisenhower.

"In God We Trust"

_____

<u>Open of the Supreme Court Sessions</u>

"God save the United States and this Honorable Court."

_____

<u>Chaplains in Government – Supreme Court ruling on it (quotes)</u>

The question of the constitutionality of government paid chaplains has already been answered by the Supreme Court in a case specifically about that issue. Here are some quotes from the majority opinion in that case.

U.S. Supreme Court
MARSH v. CHAMBERS, 463 U.S. 783 (1983)
463 U.S. 783

"The opening of sessions of legislative and other deliberative public bodies with prayer is deeply embedded in the history and tradition of this country. From colonial times through the founding of the Republic and ever since, the practice of legislative prayer has coexisted with the principles of disestablishment and religious freedom. In the very courtrooms in which the United States

112

District Judge and later three Circuit Judges heard and decided this case, the proceedings opened with an announcement that concluded, "God save the United States and this Honorable Court." The same invocation occurs at all sessions of this Court. [463 U.S. 783, 787]"

"No more is Nebraska's practice of over a century, consistent with two centuries of national practice, to be cast aside. It can hardly be thought that in the same week Members of the First Congress voted to appoint and to pay a chaplain for each House and also voted to approve the draft of the First Amendment for submission to the states, they intended the Establishment Clause of the Amendment to forbid what they had just declared acceptable. In applying the First Amendment to the states through the Fourteenth Amendment, Cantwell v. Connecticut, 310 U.S. 296 (1940), it would be incongruous to interpret that Clause as imposing more stringent [463 U.S. 783, 791] First Amendment limits on the states than the draftsmen imposed on the Federal Government."

"In light of the unambiguous and unbroken history of more than 200 years, there can be no doubt that the practice of opening legislative sessions with prayer has become part of the fabric of our society. To invoke Divine guidance on a public body entrusted with making the laws is not, in these circumstances, an "establishment" of religion or a step toward establishment; it is simply a tolerable acknowledgment of beliefs widely held among the people of this country. As Justice Douglas observed, "[w]e are a religious people whose institutions presuppose a Supreme Being." Zorach v. Clauson, 343 U.S. 306, 313 (1952)."

"Nor is the compensation of the chaplain from public funds a reason to invalidate the Nebraska Legislature's chaplaincy; remuneration is grounded in historic practice initiated, as we noted earlier, supra, at 788, by the same Congress that drafted the Establishment Clause of the First Amendment. The Continental Congress paid its chaplain, see, e. g., 6 J. Continental Cong. 887 (1776), as did some of the states, see, e. g., Debates of the Convention of Virginia 470 (June 26, 1788). Currently, many state

A Nation Under God

legislatures and the United States Congress provide compensation for their chaplains, Brief for National Conference of State Legislatures as Amicus Curiae 3; 2 U.S.C. 61d and 84-2 (1982 ed.); H. R. Res. 7, 96th Cong., 1st Sess. (1979)."

No Tax on Churches

From: Internal Revenue Service - Tax Exempt and Government Entities Exempt Organizations - tax guide for Churches and Religious Organizations (2004)

"Congress has enacted special tax laws applicable to churches, religious organizations, and ministers in recognition of their unique status in American society and of their rights guaranteed by the First Amendment of the Constitution of the United States."

Supreme Court building architecture and display

North and South Walls Courtroom Friezes:

Great Lawgivers of History – includes religious leaders Hammurabi, Moses, Solomon, Confucius, and Muhammad.

The East Pediment:

Moses and Confucius carvings are on this frieze.

Inside displays:

A statue is displayed that shows Moses coming down the

mount with the Ten Commandments.

Also, the numbers of the Ten Commandments are carved into their doors, as well as having the Ten Commandments above the head of the chief justice.

The Pledge of Allegiance

I pledge allegiance to the flag
of the United States of America
and to the country for which it stands
one nation under God, indivisible,
with liberty and justice for all.

Star Spangled Banner - National Anthem

-Fourth Verse-

Oh, thus be it ever when freemen shall stand
Between their loved home and the war's desolation;
Blest with victory and peace, may the heaven-rescued land
Praise the power that hath made and preserved us a nation!
Then conquer we must, when our cause it is just,
And this be our motto: "In God is our trust!"
And the star-spangled banner in triumph doth wave
O'er the land of the free, and the home of the brave!

The Washington Monument

The Washington Monument contains several religious quotes throughout it. Among these are...

"Praise be to God"

"Suffer the little children to come unto me and forbid them not; for such is the kingdom of God."

"Train up a child in the way he should go and when he is old, he will not depart from it."

"Search the scriptures."

"Holiness unto the Lord."

"In God we trust."

"God and our native land."

"May heaven to this union continue its beneficence."

The Jefferson Monument Quotes

"Almighty God hath created the mind free. All attempts to influence it by temporal punishments or burdens...are a departure from the plan of the Holy Author of our religion."

"The Precepts of philosophy and of the Hebrew code, laid hold of actions only. [Jesus] pushed his scrutinies into the heart of man, erected his tribunal in the regions of his thoughts, and purified the waters at the fountain head."

The Lincoln Memorial

"That this Nation, under God, shall have a new birth of freedom, and that government of the people, by the people, for the people, shall not perish from the earth."

"As was said 3000 years ago, so it still must be said, 'The judgements of the Lord are true and righteous altogether."

The Congress Building's religious expressions

The Congress building's rooms, includes an official congressional prayer room

Some Quotes in Congress Building:

"Preserve me, O God; for in thee do I put my trust."

"The New Testament according to our Lord and Savior Jesus Christ."

"In God We Trust, God With Us."

"In God We Trust" – displayed opposite the President of the Senate.

Oath of the President of the United States

The President and many other government officers say the following in their oaths upon taking term.

A Nation Under God

"So help me God"

<u>Great Seal of the United States</u>

The Great Seal of the United States is a symbol created in the first government of the United States, prior to George Washington and during the formation of the government's structure. It is currently seen on the back of United States currency. This seal contains the following words...

"annuit coeptis" - meaning "God has smiled on our undertaking."

The God that the founders put their trust of Providence in was most often the Christian God. The bible that they read was the bible Christians still read today. So, what was in this bible that convinced these founders that God was worth trusting?

This final chapter of the book provides scriptural passages of trusting God, containing the word "trust" in them. The promises and inspirations contained in them point to a God that is looking out for our wellbeing. Jeremiah 29:11 says, "For I know the thoughts that I think toward you, saith the LORD, thoughts of peace, and not of evil, to give you an expected end." This is reflective of a God who sought to die for His creation's sins, rather than condemn them, fairly, for their rebellion and pride.

Psalms 57:2-3 says, "I will cry unto God most high; unto God that performeth all things for me. He shall send from heaven, and save me from the reproach of him that would swallow me up. Selah. God shall send forth his mercy and his truth."

The term that our nation's founders used most often to refer to this Hand of God at work for us was "providence." Providence is a word with a promise. The very word providence has the word "provide" right in it. It is a promise of God to care for and direct His creation for our behalf.

God knows every day of your life, and He cannot lie. Since God knows your life and cannot lie, His promises for your protection and blessing can be relied upon. May these scriptures help inspire that reliance unto your peace and prosperity.

Scriptural Providence

1. II Samuel 22:2-4

    And he said, The Lord is my rock, and my fortress, and my deliverer;
    The God of my rock; in him will I **trust**: He is my shield, and the Horn Of my salvation, my high tower, and my refuge, my saviour; thou savest me from violence.
    I will call on the Lord, who is worthy to be praised: so shall I be saved from mine enemies.

    _____

2. II Samuel 22:31

    As for God, his way is perfect; the word of the Lord is tried: he is a buckler to all them that **trust** in him.

    _____

3. II Kings 18:5-7

    He **trusted** in the Lord God of Israel; so that after him was none like him among all the kings of Judah, nor any that were before him.
    For he clave to the Lord, and departed not from following him, but kept his commandments, which the Lord commanded Moses.
    And the Lord was with him; and he prospered whithersoever he went forth...

    _____

4.   I Chronicles 5:20

And they were helped against them, and the Hagarites were delivered into their hand, and all that were with them: for they cried to God in the battle, and he was intreated of them; because they put their **trust** in him.

_____

5.   Job 13:15-16

Though he slay me, yet will I **trust** in him: but I will maintain mine own ways before him.
He also shall be my salvation: for an hypocrite shall not come before him.

_____

6.   Job 35:12-14

There they cry, but none giveth answer, because of the pride of evil men.
Surely God will not hear vanity, neither will the Almighty regard it.
Although thou sayest thou shalt not see him, yet judgment is before him; therefore **trust** thou in him.

_____

7.   Job 39:11

Wilt thou **trust** him, because his strength is great? or wilt thou leave thy labour to him?

_____

8.   Psalms 2:12

Kiss the son, lest he be angry, and ye perish from the way, when his wrath is kindled but a little. Blessed are all they that put their **trust** in him.

---

9.   Psalms 5:11-12

But let all those that put their **trust** in thee rejoice: let them ever shout for joy, because thou defendest them: let them also that love thy name be joyful in thee.

For thou, Lord, wilt bless the righteous; with favour wilt thou compass him as with a shield.

---

10.   Psalms 7:1, 10

O Lord my God, in thee do I put my **trust**: save me from all them that persecute me, and deliver me...

My defence is of God, which saveth the upright in heart.

---

11.   Psalms 9:9-10

The Lord also will be a refuge for the oppressed, a refuge in times of trouble.

And they that know thy name will put their **trust** in thee: for thou, Lord, hast not forsaken them that seek thee.

---

12.   Psalms 11:1

In the Lord put I my **trust**: how say ye to my soul, Flee as a bird to your mountain?

_____

13. Psalms 13:5-6

But I have **trusted** in thy mercy; my heart shall rejoice in thy salvation.
I will sing unto the Lord, because he hath dealt bountifully with me.

_____

14. Psalms 16:1

Preserve me, O God: for in thee do I put my **trust**.

_____

15.   Psalms 17:7-9

Shew thy marvellous lovingkindness, O thou that savest by thy right hand them which put their **trust** in thee from those that rise up against them.
Keep me as the apple of the eye, hide me under the shadow of thy wings,
From the wicked that oppress me, from my deadly enemies, who compass me about.

_____

16. Psalms 18:2-3

The Lord is my rock, and my fortress, and my deliverer; my God, my strength, in whom I will **trust**; my buckler, and the horn of my salvation, and my high tower.

I will call upon the Lord, who is worthy to be praised: so shall I be saved from mine enemies.

---

17. Psalms 18:30

As for God, his way is perfect: the word of the Lord is tried: he is a buckler to all those that **trust** in him.

---

18. Psalms 20:7

Some **trust** in chariots, and some in horses: but we will remember the name of the Lord our God.

---

19. Psalms 21:7

For the king **trusteth** in the Lord, and through the mercy of the most High he shall not be moved.

---

20. Psalms 22:3-5

But thou art holy, O thou that inhabitest the praises of Israel.

Our fathers **trusted** in thee: they **trusted**, and thou didst deliver them.

They cried unto thee, and were delivered: they **trusted** in thee, and were not confounded.

---

21. Psalms 22:8

·   He **trusted** on the Lord that he would deliver him: let him deliver him, seeing he delighted in him.

---

22. Psalms 25:2-3

O my God, I **trust** in thee: let me not be ashamed, let not mine enemies triumph over me.

Yea, let none that wait on thee be ashamed: let them be ashamed which transgress without cause.

---

23. Psalms 26:1

Judge me, O Lord; for I have walked in mine integrity: I have **trusted** also in the Lord; therefore I shall not slide.

---

24. Psalms 28:7

The Lord is my strength and my shield; my heart **trusted** in him, and I am helped: therefore my heart greatly rejoiceth; and with my song will I praise him.

A Nation Under God

25. Psalms 31:1

In thee, O Lord, do I put my **trust**; let me never be ashamed: deliver me in thy righteousness.

_____

26. Psalms 31:5-6

Into thine hand I commit my spirit: thou hast redeemed me, O Lord God of truth.
I have hated them that regard lying vanities: but I **trust** in the Lord.

_____

27. Psalms 31:14-15

But I **trusted** in thee, O Lord: I said, Thou art my God.
My times are in thy hand: deliver me from the hand of mine enemies, and from them that persecute me.

_____

28. Psalms 31:19

Oh how great is thy goodness, which thou hast laid up for them that fear thee; which thou hast wrought for them that **trust** in thee before the sons of men!

_____

29. Psalms 32:10

Many sorrows shall be to the wicked: but he that **trusteth** in the Lord, mercy shall compass him about.

---

30. Psalms 33:21-22

For our heart shall rejoice in him, because we have **trusted** in his holy name.
Let thy mercy, O Lord, be upon us, according as we hope in thee.

---

31. Psalms 34:8

O taste and see that the Lord is good: blessed is the man that **trusteth** in him.

---

32.   Psalms 34:22

The Lord redeemeth the soul of his servants: and none of them that **trust** in him shall be desolate.

---

33. Psalms 36:7-8

How excellent is thy lovingkindness, O God! therefore the children of men put their **trust** under the shadow of thy wings.
They shall be abundantly satisfied with the fatness of thy house; and thou shalt make them drink of the river of thy pleasures.

34.   Psalms 37:3

   Trust in the Lord, and do good; so shalt thou dwell in the land, and verily thou shalt be fed.

_____

35.   Psalms 37:5

   Commit thy way unto the Lord; **trust** also in him; and he shall bring it to pass.

_____

36.   Psalms 37:39-40

   But the salvation of the righteous is of the Lord: he is their strength in the time of trouble.
   And the Lord shall help them, and deliver them: he shall deliver them from the wicked, and save them, because they **trust** in him.

_____

37.   Psalms 40:3

   And he hath put a new song in my mouth, even praise unto our God: many shall see it, and fear, and shall **trust** in the Lord.

_____

38.   Psalms 40:4

   Blessed is that man that maketh the Lord his **trust**, and

respecteth not the proud, nor such as turn aside to lies.

---

39. Psalms 44:6-8

For I will not **trust** in my bow, neither shall my sword save me.
But thou hast saved us from our enemies, and hast put them to shame that hated us.
In God we boast all the day long, and praise thy name for ever. Selah.

---

40. Psalms 52:6-7

The righteous also shall see, and fear, and shall laugh at him:
Lo, this is the man that made not God his strength; but **trusted** in the abundance of his riches, and strengthened himself in his wickedness.

---

41. Psalms 52:8-9

But I am like a green olive tree in the house of God: I **trust** in the mercy of God for ever and ever.
I will praise thee for ever, because thou hast done it: and I will wait on thy name; for it is good before thy saints.

---

42. Psalms 55:22-23

Cast thy burden upon the Lord, and he shall sustain thee: he shall never suffer the righteous to be moved.
But thou, O God, shalt bring them down into the pit of destruction: bloody and deceitful men shall not live out half their days; but I will **trust** in thee.

_____

43. Psalms 56:3

What time I am afraid, I will **trust** in thee.

_____

44. Psalms 56:4

In God I will praise his word, in God I have put my **trust**; I will not fear what flesh can do unto me.

_____

45. Psalms 56:11

In God have I put my **trust**: I will not be afraid what man can do unto me.

_____

46. Psalms 57:1

Be merciful unto me, O God, be merciful unto me: for my soul **trusteth** in thee: yea, in the shadow of thy wings will I make my refuge, until these calamities be overpast.

47. Psalms 61:3-4

For thou hast been a shelter for me, and a strong tower from the enemy.
I will abide in thy tabernacle for ever: I will **trust** in the covert of thy wings. Selah.

_____

48. Psalms 62:8

Trust in him at all times; ye people, pour out your heart before him: God is a refuge for us. Selah.

_____

49. Psalms 64:10

The righteous shall be glad in the Lord, and shall **trust** in him; and all the upright in heart shall glory.

_____

50. Psalms 71:1

In thee, O Lord, do I put my **trust**: let me never be put to confusion.

_____

51. Psalms 71:5

For thou art my hope, O Lord God: thou art my **trust** from my youth.

52. Psalms 73:28

But it is good for me to draw near to God: I have put my **trust** in the Lord God, that I may declare all thy works.

---

53. Psalms 78:21-24

Therefore the Lord heard this, and was wroth: so a fire was kindled against Jacob, and anger also came up against Israel;
Because they believed not in God, and **trusted** not in his salvation:
Though he had commanded the clouds from above, and opened the doors of heaven,
And had rained down manna upon them to eat, and had given them of the corn of heaven.

---

54. Psalms 84:12

O Lord of hosts, blessed is the man that **trusteth** in thee.

---

55. Psalms 86:2

Preserve my soul; for I am holy: O thou my God, save thy servant that **trusteth** in thee.

---

56. Psalms 91:2

I will say of the Lord, He is my refuge and my fortress: my God; in him will I **trust**.

_____

57. Psalms 91:4

He shall cover thee with his feathers, and under his wings shalt thou **trust**: his truth shall be thy shield and buckler.

_____

58. Psalms 112:6b-8

..the righteous shall be in everlasting remembrance.
He shall not be afraid of evil tidings: his heart is fixed, **trusting** in the Lord.
His heart is established, he shall not be afraid, until he see his desire upon his enemies.

_____

59. Psalms 115:9

O Israel, **trust** thou in the Lord: he is their help and their shield.

_____

60. Psalms 115:10

O house of Aaron, **trust** in the Lord: he is their help and their shield.

61. Psalms 115:11

Ye that fear the Lord, **trust** in the Lord: he is their help and their shield.

_____

62. Psalms 118:8

It is better to **trust** in the Lord than to put confidence in man.

_____

63. Psalms 118:9

It is better to **trust** in the Lord than to put confidence in princes.

_____

64. Psalms 119:41-42

Let thy mercies come also unto me, O Lord, even thy salvation, according to thy word.
So shall I have wherewith to answer him that reproacheth me: for I **trust** in thy word.

_____

65. Psalms 125:1

They that **trust** in the Lord shall be as mount Zion, which cannot be removed, but abideth for ever.

66. Psalms 141:8

But mine eyes are unto thee, O God the Lord: in thee is my **trust**; leave not my soul destitute.

_____

67. Psalms 143:8

Cause me to hear thy lovingkindness in the morning; for in thee do I **trust**: cause me to know the way wherein I should walk; for I lift up my soul unto thee.

_____

68. Psalms 144:2

My goodness, and my fortress; my high tower, and my deliverer; my shield, and he in whom I **trust**; who subdueth my people under me.

_____

69. Psalms 146:3

Put not your **trust** in princes, nor in the son of man, in whom there is no help.

_____

70. Proverbs 3:5-6

Trust in the Lord with all thine heart; and lean not unto thine own understanding.
In all thy ways acknowledge him, and he shall direct thy

paths.

_____

71. Proverbs 11:28

He that **trusteth** in his riches shall fall; but the righteous shall flourish as a branch.

_____

72. Proverbs 16:20

He that handleth a matter wisely shall find good: and whoso **trusteth** in the Lord, happy is he.

_____

73. Proverbs 28:25

He that is of a proud heart stirreth up strife: but he that putteth his **trust** in the Lord shall be made fat.

_____

74. Proverbs 28:26

He that **trusteth** in his own heart is a fool: but whoso walketh wisely, he shall be delivered.

_____

75.   Proverbs 29:25

The fear of man bringeth a snare: but whoso putteth his **trust** in the Lord shall be safe.

———————————————

76. Proverbs 30:5

Every word of God is pure: he is a shield unto them that put their **trust** in him.

———————————————

77. Isaiah 12:2

Behold, God is my salvation; I will **trust**, and not be afraid: for the Lord Jehovah is my strength and my song; he also is become my salvation.

———————————————

78. Isaiah 26:3

Thou wilt keep him in perfect peace, whose mind is stayed on thee: because he **trusteth** in thee.

———————————————

79. Isaiah 26:4

Trust ye in the Lord for ever: for in the Lord Jehovah is everlasting strength…

———————————————

80. Isaiah 50:10

Who is among you that feareth the Lord, that obeyeth the voice of his servant, that walketh in darkness, and hath no light? let him **trust** in the name of the Lord, and stay upon his God.

_____

81. Isaiah 51:5

My righteousness is near; my salvation is gone forth, and mine arms shall judge the people; the isles shall wait upon me, and on mine arm shall they **trust**.

_____

82. Isaiah 57:13

When thou criest, let thy companies deliver thee; but the wind shall carry them all away; vanity shall take them: but he that putteth his **trust** in me shall possess the land, and shall inherit my holy mountain…

_____

83. Jeremiah 7:14

Therefore will I do unto this house, which is called by my name, wherein ye **trust**, and unto the place which I gave to you and to your fathers, as I have done to Shiloh.

_____

84. Jeremiah 17:7-8

Blessed is the man that **trusteth** in the Lord, and whose hope the Lord is.

For he shall be as a tree planted by the waters, and that spreadeth out her roots by the river, and shall not see when heat cometh, but her leaf shall be green; and shall not be careful in the year of drought, neither shall cease from yielding fruit.

---

85. Jeremiah 39:18

For I will surely deliver thee, and thou shalt not fall by the sword, but thy life shall be for a prey unto thee: because thou hast put thy **trust** in me, saith the Lord.

---

86. Jeremiah 49:11

Leave thy fatherless children, I will preserve them alive; and let thy widows **trust** in me.

---

87. Daniel 3:28

Then Nebuchadnezzar spake, and said, Blessed be the God of Shadrach, Meshach, and Abednego, who hath sent his angel, and delivered his servants that **trusted** in him, and have changed the king's word, and yielded their bodies, that they might not serve nor worship any god, except their own God.

---

88. Nahum 1:7

The Lord is good, a strong hold in the day of trouble; and he knoweth them that **trust** in him.

---

89. Matthew 12:18-21

Behold my servant, whom I have chosen; my beloved, in whom my soul is well pleased: I will put my spirit upon him, and he shall shew judgment to the Gentiles.

He shall not strive, nor cry; neither shall any man hear his voice in the streets.

A bruised reed shall he not break, and smoking flax shall he not quench, till he send forth judgment unto victory.

And in his name shall the Gentiles **trust**.

---

90. Romans 15:12

And again, Esaias saith, There shall be a root of Jesse, and he that shall rise to reign over the Gentiles; in him shall the Gentiles **trust**.

---

91. II Corinthians 1:9

But we had the sentence of death in ourselves, that we should not **trust** in ourselves, but in God which raiseth the dead...

---

92. II Corinthians 1:10

Who delivered us from so great a death, and doth deliver: in whom we **trust** that he will yet deliver us...

_____

93. II Corinthians 3:4-5

And such **trust** have we through Christ to God-ward:
Not that we are sufficient of ourselves to think any thing as of ourselves; but our sufficiency is of God.

_____

94. Ephesians 1:12-13

That we should be to the praise of his glory, who first **trusted** in Christ.
In whom ye also **trusted**, after that ye heard the word of truth, the gospel of your salvation: in whom also after that ye believed, ye were sealed with that holy Spirit of promise...

_____

95. Philippians 2:19

But I **trust** in the Lord Jesus to send Timotheus shortly unto you, that I also may be of good comfort, when I know your state.

_____

96. Philippians 2:24

But I **trust** in the Lord that I also myself shall come shortly.

97. I Timothy 4:10

For therefore we both labour and suffer reproach, because we **trust** in the living God, who is the Saviour of all men, specially of those that believe.

_____

98. I Timothy 5:5-6

Now she that is a widow indeed, and desolate, **trusteth** in God, and continueth in supplications and prayers night and day. But she that liveth in pleasure is dead while she liveth.

_____

99. I Timothy 6:17

Charge them that are rich in this world, that they be not highminded, nor **trust** in uncertain riches, but in the living God, who giveth us richly all things to enjoy...

_____

100. Philemon 1:22

But withal prepare me also a lodging: for I **trust** that through your prayers I shall be given unto you.

Source Citations and Research Links

Online Resource Citations

Letters to / from Congress:
http://memory.loc.gov/ammem/amlaw/lawhome.html

Military Hymns:
Army - http://bands.army.mil/history/music/armysong.asp
Navy - http://www.chinfo.navy.mil/navpalib/traditions/music/anchor1.html
Air Force - http://www.usafa.af.mil/ccp/afhymn.htm
Marines - http://www.usmcpress.com/heritage/marine_hymn.htm
Coast Guard - http://www.uscg.mil/hq/g-cp/history/faqs/uscg_hymn.html

Official Government Documents and Info:
http: //www.aclj.org/resources/
http://thomas.loc.gov/

Presidential Denominational Information:
http://www.adherents.com/
http://www.whitehouse.gov/history/presidents/

Presidential Inaugural Addresses:
http://www.bartleby.com/
http://www.whitehouse.gov/history/presidents/
http://memory.loc.gov/ammem/pihtml/pihome.html

Stars and Stripes (Paris, France) WWI prayers – 1918-1919
A Prayer of Victory - January 3, 1919, Vol. 1 No. 48 page 4
A Sister's Prayer - June 14, 1918, Vol. 1 No. 19, page 8
A Veteran's Prayer - June 14, 1918, Vol. 1 No. 19, page 8
A Chaplain's Prayer - June 21, 1918, Vol. 1 No. 20 page 4
A Soldier's Prayer - May 31, 1918, Vol. 1 No. 17 page 5
A Battle Prayer - November 29, 1918, Vol. 1 No. 43 page 4

State Constitutions:
http://www.constitution.org/cons/usstcons.htm
http://dir.yahoo.com/government/law/constitutional/constitutions/
http://lcweb.loc.gov/global/state/stategov.html

Supreme Court building architecture info
The East Pediment
- http://www.supremecourtus.gov/about/eastpediment.pdf

Courtroom Friezes: North and South Walls
-http://www.supremecourtus.gov/about/north&southwalls.pdf

Thanksgiving (and other) Proclamations:
http://memory.loc.gov/ammem/rbpehtml/pehome.html
http://www.pilgrimhall.org/ThanxProc.htm
http://www.whitehouse.gov/holiday/thanksgiving/

Washington Territory's first telegraph to Washington D. C. – 1864
http://memory.loc.gov/ammem/alhtml/malhome.html

Wyoming National Day of Prayer Proclamation
http://wyoming.gov/governor/press_releases/execorder/2000/text_prayer.html

Year of the Bible Proclamation - 1983
http://www.reagan.utexas.edu/resource/speeches/1983/20383b.htm

Print Resource Citations

Chaplains in Government – Supreme Court ruling
MARSH v. CHAMBERS, 463 U.S. 783 (1983) 463 U.S. 783

Constitutional Convention – 1787 – Benjamin Franklin's words
Federer, William J. (1994) America's God and Country Encyclopedia of Quotations.
Coppell, TX: FAME Publishing, Inc. pp 248-249

Gettysburg Address – Abraham Lincoln – 1863:
Presidential Prayer Team Devotional (1st ed.).(2003). Nashville, TN: J Countryman. p
34.

Monument and Memorial Quotes:
Federer, William J. (1994) America's God and Country Encyclopedia of Quotations.
Coppell, TX: FAME Publishing, Inc.

My Country 'Tis of Thee – Samuel Francis Smith – 1832
Presidential Prayer Team Devotional (1st ed.).(2003). Nashville, TN: J Countryman. p
39.

No Tax on churches
Tax Exempt and Government Entities Exempt Organizations - tax guide for Churches
and Religious Organizations (2004) - Internal Revenue Service

Star Spangled Banner
God Bless America (1st ed.).(1999).Grand Rapids, MI: Zondervan. p 203

State Motto and Presidential Political Party Information:
The Oxford Essential Desk Reference (1st ed.).(2001). New York, NY: Berkley Books.
pp. 292-293, 232-233.

11948651R0009

Made in the USA
Lexington, KY
12 November 2011